Publication Information

First Edition

First Printing, 2016

Library of Congress Cataloging-in-Publication Data

Holland, Deb

Leaders My Leaders! Your Journey to Awesomeness / Deb Holland - 1st ed.

Library of Congress Control Number: 2016905759

CreateSpace Independent Publishing Platform, North Charleston, SC

ISBN 13: 978-1530499038

ISBN 10: 1530499038

1) Leadership, 2) Team building, 3) Organizational health, 4) Winning culture, 5) Business management

Disclaimer

All characters appearing in this work are fictitious. Any resemblance to real people, living or dead, is entirely coincidental. All locations / settings are also fictitious. Teaching points and story examples are fictionalized, composite representations of the experiences I've had over the course of my working life. None of them depict any specific individual or organization at any time in my working history.

I list several excellent organizations / awesome individuals in this book as resources. This does not imply their endorsement of me or my work. Their inclusion is solely my endorsement of them and the difference they make in people's lives.

Photographs © Annie Rubens, used with permission

Workbook design by Fran Schiesl, Spot-on-Graphics

Dedication

To all the employees who have suffered under bad bosses. My heart goes out to you. I understand the staggering losses you've faced. Time. Money. Energy. Peace. Health. Marriage. Friends. Family. Hope. And for some, life itself. You will always be in my prayers. I am dedicating the rest of my life to helping leaders get it right for all of us.

Prayer for God to Bless Our Work Together

Dear God, I pray that every leader comes to know you. Because when people know You, it changes *everything.* Thank you for the blessing and honor of writing this book. May it help raise up a generation of leaders who conduct themselves according to principle. Who become mighty stewards of the power entrusted to them. Teach them to love their teams and always do right by them. Amen!

Gratitudes

Annie Rubens, for her awesome photography, editing, encouragement, and inspiration.

Fran Schiesl, for her outstanding graphic design, editing, and belief in me.

All of my teams over the course of my life. You know who you are. Whether it was in class, after school, or at a job site, it was a privilege to lead you. Nothing made me happier than watching you grow and succeed. I still love you, I still pray for you, and I greatly look forward to watching you write the next chapter of your own dreams. You will be forever in my heart.

The Door County Sled Dogs, a 501(c)3, all rescued dogs/all volunteer organization, are a recreational dog sled team whose mission is education and fun - for children, adults, and families year-round!

This amazingly wonderful and hard working team began with Mushers Rick Desotelle and Bonnie Ulrich (retired educators) training in the city of Milwaukee and outback areas of Door County. After much volunteerism and local interest about rescues, dog-powered sports, good pet care and obedience as well as leadership and

team qualities, the DCSD's partnered up with the Milwaukee County Parks and other civic groups to provide outstanding presentations and fun-filled rides and other experiences. Although the team is not a general racing team, they do race for charities such as the Make-a-Wish foundation and Adopt-a-Husky. Proceeds to sustain the team and all of their activities is entirely dependent on working to sustain themselves and sponsorships. All of your donations go directly to the care of the RESCUES. Please consider helping these amazingly wonderful sled dogs. Musher Rick and Boo Boo are featured below:

Special thanks to the Door County Sled Dogs for granting us permission to feature their information and pictures in the book.
Woof Woof Arooooo for the Huskies and their Mushers!

Table Of Contents

<u>Introduction</u>

We have a leadership crisis in this country, and I am on a mission to fix it. Leaders wield enormous power over the lives of their teams and organizations. Some of them handle that responsibility beautifully. Others are a disaster. I've been working for over three decades now. During that time, I've had the pleasure of working for awesome leaders who treated their people right and accomplished great things. I've also had the heartbreak of working for highly dysfunctional managers who deliberately inflicted as much damage on people as they possibly could. As a result, they compromised missions, ruined work environments, and left untold destruction in their wake. You know the kind of leader I'm talking about. They're the type whose negative impact has a huge ripple effect beyond the workplace itself. They cost people their health, rob them of their joy, strain their most important relationships, and sometimes strip away all hope. People die because of these leaders. Marriages fall apart. Families break up. Bodies break down. Minds and hearts fall into despondency and despair. You've seen these leaders in action. They act with impunity and get away with as much as they can, for as long as they can. They sacrifice others for their own personal gain.

Some of the biggest headline news stories of the last two decades involve leaders across all industries and sectors who crashed headlong into their day of accountability. Don't let this be you! Whether you are an aspiring leader who wants to form habits of excellence from the start, a mid-career leader who is looking to step up their game, or an executive who wants to make sure their performance grows to the elite level, this book can help you. And this book is for one more very special category of leaders: those who have messed up and are willing to do something about it. If that's you, then you are holding a plan for redemption in your hands. You need this book more than anyone else. It is not too late for you. Change is always possible and is literally just one good decision away.

Leaders hold an awesome, sacred responsibility to achieve missions, grow teams, and develop individuals. Too many of them are busy accomplishing anything but. Too many of them treat their organizations and teams as commodities in their quest for personal gain. Too many of them treat their people as discardable. The abuse or neglect of power carries grave consequences. **Leaders are spiritually responsible for the impact they have on those under their command.** Leaders who focus on anything other than improving themselves, the team, the organization, and ultimately the communities in which they operate will eventually have their choices come back to haunt them. We all reap what we sow. The clock of accountability is ticking. What kind of leader are you? Are your people suffering or succeeding? What kind of results are you getting? Are you making the myriad sacrifices required to successfully lead a team? Or are you leaving a trail of blown missions and broken people in your wake? Be honest.

Leadership magnifies flaws. Leaders who choose to put themselves through the necessary discomfort of a personal growth plan evolve into leaders who are a powerful, positive force to reckon with. Leaders who choose to sacrifice their team on the altar of their own dysfunction, will eventually encounter a rebellion that forces them to grow and evolve. If they're lucky. The news tells us that some leaders don't get a second chance. Some of them get fired. Some end up on the nightly news. Some end up behind bars. None of them emerge unscathed.

Here's the beauty of this book: no matter what kind of leader you are, you can improve outcomes with the mission and the team. Even if your team hates you, even if you've lost all control and your world is crashing down around you, it still isn't too late. The choice you make, *right now*, in the quiet of your own mind and heart, determines your fate as a leader. All leaders need a self-development program. I have a giant heart of compassion for leaders and I am devoting the rest of my life to helping them learn how to get things right in these four critical areas: self, team, organization, and community.

Leaders rising up and taking action to transform their environments from dysfunctional hovels to healthy, productive environments is of vital importance in living rooms and boardrooms all across the country. Our workforce is at your mercy. The viability and vitality of our organizations lies entirely in your hands. *Your contribution to our nation will never exceed the boundaries of your character.* Your mission will not succeed beyond the constraints created by the weakest leader on your roster.

Leaders my leaders, it's time! Time to get real. Time to get serious. Time to wrest back control from those who follow the darkness. Time to protect those who are counting on you. It's time to rise up with boldness and seize this opportunity to make a quantum leap to the next level. Arise, and let your light shine!

Part One: Leadership of the Self

Leaders my leaders, I am going to speak to you from the heart. I care deeply about you. I also care deeply about your team. I'm asking you to listen with your heart. It won't matter how much you intellectually understand the words written in this book if you don't really comprehend them with your heart. This book is intended to give you new information and a fresh perspective. If you're already scoffing, then you need this book more than anyone else.

If you picked up this book, then chances are that you're either a fantastic leader who is always interested in building their skills, or you are the kind of leader who knows deep down that you have room for improvement. Maybe a lot of improvement. Maybe you've even messed up so bad you think you're beyond hope. If you're willing to take a hard look at the reality of your situation, and then get right to work doing something about it, you can overcome whatever obstacle you're facing.

Let me share with you a few truths about leadership. It's a tough business. It's not comfortable. Nor is it supposed to be. It's not about you. It's about the team. If you have to make a choice between one individual and the team, pick the team. Every time. You are there as a human shield. You are there to absorb the hits on behalf of the team. You are there to maintain order, to inspire, educate, entertain, counsel, console, comfort, build up, look after, make sacrifices for, love, encourage, care about, and hold accountable your team. All that is on you. It's a big job. But it's worth it. Because guiding a group of people who share your values towards accomplishing a mission for the common good, well, that's the good stuff in life. For every moment their quirks drive you crazy, they'll repay you with a thousand moments of pride at watching them grow and accomplish more than they thought possible. Become more than they thought possible. For every time the goofy troubles they get themselves into make you curse under your breath, there will be moments that take your breath away because they pulled off something amazing.

This is what it means to be a leader, to serve alongside a team. You're there with them, and for them. In every circumstance. You are the one they are looking to. You are the one who holds so much of their well-being in your hands. If that doesn't simultaneously terrify, excite, and awe you, then you have some serious work ahead of you. The skills of leadership can be learned. But having a good heart cannot. If your heart isn't right towards your people and your organization, then you are on a collision course with the consequences of your bad choices. If this is you, then your only hope is to let your heart be transformed. This book can help you do that. Keep reading.

Leadership begins with you. If you're chaotic or dysfunctional, then you're going to do damage. It really is that simple. You have to lead yourself to make good choices first before you can expect that from your team. Every day you are sowing seeds that you will harvest later. What is your harvest going to be like? Will it be robust, with just a few unavoidable weeds mixed in? Or will it be mostly weeds, with a few inadvertent good things mixed in? The bottom line is, if you are making healthy choices, you and your team are going to have a bountiful harvest. But if you are making bad choices, then you are going to face those consequences, especially now that you know better. Leading yourself first brings you peace, your team hope, and your organization good results. You will become an upstanding member of the community. You will respect yourself. You will honor yourself and the role you have been gifted with.

Section one of this book is going to teach you the three key aspects of self-leadership: maturity, integrated wholeness, and sustainable life practices. All three are essential to building a foundation of bedrock rather than quicksand under your leadership. For those wise enough to choose to build on bedrock, their leadership will stand the test of time and all kinds of weather. For those who foolishly build on quicksand, there will come a day when the wind or the rain erodes what was never strong to begin with, and swallows the leader up into their own self-created darkness. I've seen it happen time and time again, and it is never pretty.

I have one more powerful choice to point out to you. The very best leaders I've ever known all had one thing in common. They were coming from a spiritual perspective. Notice I didn't say they all came from the same religion. Or attended any particular church. Or read from the same version of scripture. Or worshipped in the same ways. If you just clucked your tongue or rolled your eyes, this next part is especially for you. If you and God aren't on speaking terms, you need to work through that. If you are at war with God then it will be impossible for you or your team to have peace. For the purposes of this book I am not defining peace as the absence of trouble. I am defining it as the unshakeable faith in yourself and your team that tells you that no matter what happens, you will be able to figure it out. Together. It all begins with you. God is the only one who can transform you. My role is to put words on the page that make you think. That lead you to making better choices. God takes care of everything else that you need. His mercy is fresh and new each day. All you have to do is ask for it. If you still aren't moved to even consider connecting with God and you insist on going it alone, this book can still help you. But as a friend who loves and cares about you, I'm telling you right now that if you exclude God and spirituality from your leadership, then you will be appointed *to* your position but will never know the blessings of being divinely anointed *for* your position.

As should be abundantly clear by now, I love leadership, I love my teams, and I love God. That's a powerful combination I wouldn't trade for anything else. I've sacrificed much as I've served in various leadership capacities over the years. I've borne immense costs. I've also experienced untold joy as those who once served under my command moved on to bigger and better purposes in their own lives. I've had the pleasure of accomplishing missions that truly made a big difference in people's lives. I've also known the pain of making stupid mistakes, and had flaws I needed to overcome. It hasn't been easy, but it is extraordinarily worth it. This is my bedrock: I follow God, my teams follow me, and I serve Him and them. It's an awesome spiral of success that reaches ever upwards. They see and feel the difference this makes. Friends, I am inviting you to make the same kind of difference. Get your foundation and your priorities right by choosing to humble yourself to God as you understand Him, and watch the supernatural transformation that will take place. If you do that, you'll be counted among the greatest leaders of your generation.

<u>Chapter One: Personal Maturity</u>

Integrity is not the most important trait for a leader to have, maturity is. Mature people have hallmark traits that can be relied upon. Mature people get the best possible results from themselves and others. They have evolved to their highest level of functioning, living, and loving. Then they seek to learn and grow even more. These folks are in balance, have a great perspective, and an excellent attitude. They are fully accountable, and make mindful, intentional choices. They have a profoundly positive ripple impact on the world.

Immature leaders cause a lot of destruction. They may not have one of the major dysfunctions we'll talk about in the next chapter, but they also haven't grown up enough to meet their current responsibilities well. Some of them are immature because they lack an example that showed them what maturity looks like in daily life. Others are proudly immature because they have no interest in self-development, and they benefit too much from their bad behavior. Eventually however, their choices will catch up with them. Immature leaders are forced to grow up in a hurry when something happens that they aren't able to escape or laugh off. Then they regret not having chosen to develop maturity when they still had control over the process.

The bottom line is that life will grow you up. The same is true of leadership. The path of self-discipline is rougher at the start, but allows you the time and space to grow at your own pace and in your own way. It becomes a comfort and one of your greatest allies throughout the course of the rest of your life. Those who don't choose self-discipline however, have a more carefree start but a much tougher landing later on. Usually by then, someone or something has intervened. At that point the path to maturity is prescribed and must be accomplished in a compressed timeframe. Someone else is setting the goals, making the decisions, and then you are stuck carrying out their plan.

The benefits of choosing to intentionally develop maturity are clear: better results for you and everyone else. You'll find inner peace and discover the ability to wisely handle whatever comes your way. But please keep in mind that none of us is perfect. No one will have every trait listed below. Nor will they use the traits they do have perfectly in every circumstance. The key is to keep growing.

Traits of an Immature Person	Traits of a Mature Person
Highly disrespectful, strips people of their dignity	Treats others with dignity and respect
Reacts, at the mercy of every changing circumstance in their life	Responds from a values based place that dictates how they choose to act regardless of the circumstance
Shows off to impress others, whether it is bragging about what they have, or treating others poorly to gain social capital	Reaches out to authentically connect with other people
Ridicules others	Protects others
Sacrifices others for personal gain	Makes strategic sacrifices that advance the common good

Arrogant	Humble
Believes everyone thinks just like they do	Realizes the world is a big place with a vast diversity of beliefs
Worldview restricted to their personal opinion, they are closed minded	Open minded and their worldview continually expands as they meet new people and have new experiences
Revengeful, hold grudges, punish people	Stand up for themselves but don't seek vengeance
Drives wedges between people	Builds bridges between people
Lies, cheats, and/or steals	Acts with honesty and integrity
Feels entitled	Believes they need to earn what they get
Shirks responsibility	Embraces responsibility, even in the tough times
Does what feels good in the moment	Does the right thing, even when its really hard
Tears others down, makes them feel bad	Uplifts others, gives them hope
Never forgives	Intentionally begins the process of forgiveness so they can be free, doesn't matter how long it takes or how messy it gets
Never repents or makes amends	Takes full accountability and makes things right as quickly as possible when they mess up, focuses on doing better the next time
Never examines their own behavior	Chooses values and principles in advance, and reviews their behavior regularly to ensure they are living in accordance with them
Cruel	Compassionate

Meddles in other people's business	Unless it involves safety or well-being, honors the right of self-determination
Wastes time on frivolous activities	Thoughtfully chooses and pursues activities that are essential to them
Plays God in the lives of others	Respects and submits to God
Deliberately withholds power, knowledge, or other resources to keep people in a one down position	Actively shares resources to facilitate advancement for everyone involved
Believes they are smarter than everyone else	Understands that intelligence lies on a continuum, with some being ahead of them, and some behind
Believes they are superior to everyone else	Understands that no one is any better or worse than anyone else
Jealous	Happy for others when they succeed
Has to be disciplined by others	Exhibits tremendous self-discipline
Callous	Empathetic
Unable to deal with their own emotions, so they try to squash other's emotions	Has mastered their own emotions enough to hold space for others who are having a tough time, without shutting them down or shaming them
Takes other's emotions personally, easily offended, easily wounded	Rarely takes the emotions of others personally, even more difficult to offend or wound
Deliberately disruptive	Deliberately calming, tries to bring peace and order to the situation

Thinks its fun to scare, hurt, bully, or harass other people	Recognizes the vulnerability in all of us, holds it as sacred, protects it
Dominates, overpowers, or sabotages others	Works collaboratively with other people, has no hidden agenda, lets others shine
Active shadow side, different in public than they are in private	Congruence in behavior regardless of where they are
Doesn't keep confidences, breaks trust	Trustworthy
Chases pleasure	Sets and pursues meaningful goals
Lives by their moods and whims	Sets and lives by carefully chosen priorities
Treats people harshly	Treats people with kindness
Worships false idols: self, relationships, money, substances, activities, etc	Worships the God of their understanding, comprehends that there is a power much greater than themselves

To help illustrate the concepts above, we're going to draw a comparison between two leaders, one who is mature, and one who is not. In the chapters that follow, we will continue the story of these leaders with the new material we learn along the way.

The Story of Ichabod

Ichabod was born into an alcoholic family. His father never found recovery. He was a sensitive child, who was picked on and experienced much shame and pain. As he grew, he became increasingly callous and disruptive of other people. He eventually found himself on the wrong side of the law, and was forced to experience consequences he didn't like. However, he didn't take that opportunity to grow up. He met the prescribed requirements, but was really just playing along. As soon as he was out from under the control of others, he went right back to his hard partying, fast living ways. He also blamed others for the state of his life. He developed a great deal of rage he had an increasingly difficult time controlling. It leaked out of him at the slightest provocation, at things that had nothing to do with him at all. He felt the need to constantly remind others of his own importance. He deliberately withheld what others needed from him, so that he could remind them he was in charge. Predictably, he ended up divorced and found himself in yet another situation in which his actions were dictated by someone else. He didn't take that opportunity to grow up either.

He didn't bother taking a look at his own behavior to see how he had contributed to his own problems. He simply developed more rage. He also started to develop serious health problems. He just kept adding to the list of people he blamed for his circumstances. His rage grew even greater, and so much of it was spilling out of him that more and more people avoided him. Unless they thought they could get something from him. Blind to his own vulnerabilities, he was manipulated by people who quickly figured out that stroking his ego was their ticket to special privileges. He was also highly manipulative, and had managed to cut enough shady deals to be promoted to a team leader position. He sacrificed his team for his own personal gain, always choosing to protect himself at their expense. He would call them foul names behind closed doors, and then schmooze them to their faces. The mature people saw right through him, and he hated them for it. He began pitting his cronies against them, and enjoyed the spectacle of the chaos that followed.

He was wildly insecure, jealous, and begrudging of other people's success. He couldn't relate to accomplishing goals on their merits. He rarely earned what he got, and felt entitled to even more. He was deeply in debt because he chased women, took vacations he couldn't afford, and had a stockpile of toys that he added to regularly. He saw himself as a great success, and other people as losers. He thought he was invincible, and behaved with impunity. Right up until he once again ran headlong into the consequences of his choices. He found himself under other people's control yet again, and they prescribed his actions. He was furious but couldn't escape the mess he was in. His career stalled. He was widely reviled as sleazy. His girlfriend left him. His dream of becoming a father looked like it might never come true. His health was crashing. His rage became uncontainable as he blamed more and more people for his problems. But he still didn't take the opportunity to grow up.

The Story of Emma

Emma was born into an addicted family. Her father never found recovery. She believed in God from as far back as she could remember. When she got a little older, she went to church even if her parents didn't. It was her sanctuary. There was chaos at home, and she was bullied at school. As she grew, she had plenty of anger about her situation. She went through a self-destructive phase. But when she reached young adulthood, she woke up one day and realized she was becoming just like her family. She made a decision to get help. Even though it was really hard at first, she stuck with it. She watched her peers continue to party, live at home, and quit jobs whenever they felt like it. She lived on her own, in spartan conditions. She worked at entry level jobs that paid barely enough to make the bills. She returned to her apartment each day exhausted, but had the self-discipline to take the time to work on her goals. She was determined to learn the skills it took to live a better life. Determined to become a responsible adult. She was by no means perfect. She still made mistakes, and backslid. Sometimes she made really bad choices. But she always came back to a place of resetting her values and priorities, and trying again. It took a long time to overcome all that had been done to her, and to clean up the messes she herself had made along the way. But she stuck with that too. She blamed others only long enough to face the truth of the situation, and then gave it to God. She set an intention to forgive, and that was perhaps the hardest thing of all. Gradually, her life improved. She met a good man, married, and had children.

She was blessed with increasingly responsible positions at work until one day, she had her own team to lead. She was thrilled, and took her responsibilities very seriously. She was determined to get this part of her life right too. She treated her people well. Sometimes she made mistakes, but she corrected them and got right back on track. She had a huge heart of compassion for her people, and they quickly learned she would listen to them without judgment. She protected them to the best of her ability, was authentic with them, and worked to help them accomplish their dreams.

They trusted her because she had earned it. Their working relationships flourished, and their team grew strong. They knew she would hold each of them accountable, starting with herself. They faced the usual stresses and struggles of group dynamics, but she made sure they came out the other side of it with problems solved and relationships preserved. They set the standard for productivity. The mission of the organization was safe in their hands. Yet despite their great success, none of them rested on their laurels. She had taught them that accountability never ends, and they stayed mindful of living up to the values and priorities they had set for themselves.

Emma was happy, and at peace. She looked back at the years she had spent making herself learn how to grow up, and she was so grateful. She looked around and realized that some of her peers were still filled with immaturity despite their advancing age. They had mocked the pivotal moments in their lives rather than be transformed by them. She saw them paying the price with their health, their marriages, and their financial well-being. She thanked God every day that she had already done so much hard work on herself, and that she didn't have to start from scratch at her age. She had tremendous compassion for those who still struggled, and she prayed for them regularly.

<u>Chapter One Exercises</u>

- ✓ Go through the list above and highlight the mature traits you already possess.
- ✓ Take a look at the traits you did not highlight. Pick two or three you want to work on first, and write them in here:

_____

_____

- ✓ Write a brief action plan for how you'll develop each one of those traits:

_____

_____

_____

<u>Chapter Two: Integrated Wholeness</u>

You will never reach your full potential as a leader unless you become an integrated, whole person. You will have the best possible impact, and also have the most inner peace, once you do the work required to fully develop yourself as a person. There are a lot of excellent resources out there about how to accomplish this goal. Regardless of what kind of issue you face, there is hope for you. There are a wealth of options for getting help with specific problems. In this digital age, there is no excuse for not finding free or low-cost resources to make progress on areas that are holding you back. Your local library system can also offer you life-changing CDs, DVDs, and other materials at no cost whatsoever. You don't have to have a lot of money or spend years in therapy to overcome the trouble in your life. If you can afford therapy and feel it might be useful to you, then by all means make use of it. But if you don't have the money to spend to get yourself some help, then make the most of the free resources that are available. That includes church, sports, music, the arts, or a lot of other rewarding activities in life. Find something healthy that brings you happiness and peace, that challenges you, and gives you a sense of connection. You'll grow in those types of environments, and good changes you make in one area will help to improve others.

The bottom line is, we all have issues we are dealing with, and we all have baggage of one kind or another from the past. Maybe you grew up in dire circumstances, or maybe you've made such bad mistakes that you feel broken and resigned to a lesser life. Once you're an adult, it really doesn't matter whose fault something was, what matters is what you do to move past it. You will miss out on opportunities if you remain fragmented or compartmentalized. Unless you've faced your own darkness, you'll have blind spots that will be readily apparent to others. You'll have an inner angst that will gnaw at you, and that will show up in a variety of ways in your life. People want to help those who are sincerely doing their own work. They don't want to help people who refuse to live in reality, or who have a bad attitude. Be fully awake to your own life, in its entirety. Face it, fix it, and flourish.

In addition to basic resources, there are also some outstanding self-development programs that can help you achieve transformative growth and an elite level of performance. Mark Divine is one of my all-time favorites. His Unbeatable Mind and SealFit programs are unrivaled. You can find them online at www.unbeatablemind.com and www.sealfit.com. The work of Jon Kabat-Zinn on living mindfully is extraordinary. If you do an internet search you will find multiple options for connecting with his work. So is the work of Joel Osteen (www.joelosteen.com), Joyce Meyer (www.joycemeyer.org), and Bishop T.D. Jakes (www.tdjakes.org). The point is to find a teacher you respect and learn all you can from them. Take what you think will work for you and apply it, and leave the rest. The goal is to let someone guide you to your own best growth.

Now let's talk about the major issues that can hold an individual back personally and professionally. It is essential to determine what type of impairment is compromising the ability to function in a healthy way. While problems will vary by degree and individual, there are five main categories of impairments: addiction, mental health, criminal activity, drama stagers, and immaturity.

1. **Addiction**. The individual may be addicted to a substance or activity. Or they may be involved in other people's addictions. Or they may have grown up in family that had an addict in it. Active addiction issues encroach on the work environment. The addict may be using their substance or engaging in their activity on the premises, at lunch, or on company time. Or they may keep the active use out of the workplace, but the effects still cause significant problems. Signs can

include poor attendance, lack of productivity, being preoccupied to the point of distraction, mood swings based on getting their fix, hostile interactions with others, lying, cheating, stealing, secretive behavior, and punishment for those who do not help cover the addict's tracks.

In much the same way, people who grew up in an addicted family and who have never dealt with those issues also show classic behavioral traits that disrupt the work environment, often creating a toxic undercurrent that erodes trust, productivity, and mission accomplishment. It also does a lot of damage to healthy people, in much the same way that a daily dose of poison would hurt a healthy person. There are some great lists online about the behaviors that are commonly seen in adult children of addicted families. We don't have time to go into them in detail today, but in general it comes down to a person living by rigid rules and roles, with severe consequences for anyone who steps outside that restricted world. The goal with every trait, rule, and role is to protect the addict from the consequences of his/her own behavior. The addict shoves off their responsibility to the rest of the family, and rather than taking responsibility for themselves, they force their family to take the responsibility for them. It is crazy making for people who aren't actually responsible for something, to be required to take responsibility for it. There is a lot of hysteria about this. If someone doesn't play their part, the addicted family acts as if it is a matter of life or death. They will stop at nothing to make the healthy person look like the sick person. There is enormous desperation to hide the truth.

The addicted family creates a highly distorted world for everyone in it. It's not always clear to the people inside that system, what is real and what is distorted. When the children of these families grow up and enter the work force, if they have never dealt with these issues, they will end up functioning in their teams the way they functioned in their family. Leaders will end up creating workplaces that function like their addicted family. They will select a narrative for themselves, perhaps that they need to be taken care of (the victim). This translates to a mandate that their employees keep secrets for them so they don't face consequences for their behavior. If there is a staff member who grew up in an addicted family and never dealt with their issues either, they will leap to the defense of the leader at any cost (the rescuer).

Healthy employees who have dealt with their issues and make good choices and don't buy into the sick rules or roles they are supposed to play are branded the enemy (the villains.) What happens in these situations is a battle develops between the healthy people wanting to do their jobs, and the unhealthy people wanting to stage a drama each day. The "victims" send out distress signals to the "rescuers" and together they fight to vanquish the "villains." They replicate in the work environment what took place in their living room growing up. This causes mass damage to people and missions.

2. **Mental health**. The individual may have a psychological or emotional issue they are dealing with. This can range from an acute reaction to life stress, to full blown episodes of mental illness. Signs can include erratic behavior, unpredictable moods, high levels of conflict with other people, or a loose grip on reality. It is important to distinguish between situational stress that exists due to an external challenge in only one environment, versus problematic behavior that is generated by the individual and is pervasive across environments.

We all face situational stress. Health problems, family issues, money troubles, or other types of difficulties can throw anyone temporarily off their game. It's possible to have more than one life problem at once, and be in a highly stressed state, but again it is temporary. The trouble is coming from the stressors overwhelming the coping skills or other resources the person has to resolve them. The pressure is coming from the outside of the person, and they are doing their best to adapt to it.

Mental health issues are internal. The pressure comes from inside the person. They tend to experience the same kinds of problems in all their environments, including work, family and personal life. This is not to say they are bad people. It is important only in terms of trying to figure out how to deal with the impact on the work environment. If you are dealing with someone with a true mental illness, it may be that they aren't able to respond well to attempts to work towards more acceptable behavior. People under situational stress who are advised about the impact of their behavior/attitude on the team will generally pause and realize the problems are bleeding over into work. They will at least make a good faith effort to get themselves back on track well enough to function in the work environment. They are capable of seeing their behavior accurately, understanding its impact, and then making positive change. People with true mental illness however, may lack the capacity for that kind of insight, empathy, and behavioral adjustment. There is a lot of good information online about how specific disorders affect people, if you are interested in learning more about signs and symptoms. These people typically want to do a good job, but have organic issues that make it really tough for them.

3. **Criminal activity**. We can't pretend this doesn't happen just because it's an uncomfortable topic for some people to think about. We like to see the best in people, but it's necessary for us to face the harsh reality that some people make choices in their lives to become involved in illegal activities. Some of these people will engage in illegal behavior while at work. They may steal from the company, gain access to confidential information and use it for personal gain, exploit customers, or even use their workplace as an operational outpost for their criminal enterprise. Even if people are involved in criminal activity only outside of work, the effects of that can still greatly impact the environment. Signs can include sudden unexplained improvement in socioeconomic status, secretive behavior, bragging about their exploits, co-workers witnessing suspicious transactions, or association with questionable people. These people will have zero interest in changing their behavior because they are profiting from it too much. All the advanced communication skills workshops in the world won't help when dealing with this kind of issue. These people don't honor the spirit or mission of a workplace, they corrode it. If they perceive someone as interfering with their activities, they can turn dangerous or even violent.

4. **Drama stagers**. For those of you who have not yet read the work of Dr. Alan Godwin, I highly recommend his book "How to Deal With Your People Problems" (2011, www.dralangodwin.com). Dr. Godwin gives us the incredible gift of teaching us skills about how to deal with people who have a hidden manipulative agenda, or who are simply so wrapped up in themselves they do not care what the impact of their behavior is on other people. His work fills in the missing piece for those of us who have sat through workshop after workshop on dealing with difficult people and then left saying "this doesn't work with the people I am dealing with." You can read Dr. Godwin's work for the details, but for now I am going to add my perspective on the conversation he so eloquently started.

Drama stagers create particularly crazy making environments. Their behavior differs from people who grew up in addicted families. When adult children learn the telltale signs of how their addicted family impacted them, their life suddenly makes sense in a brand new way. They are generally grateful for the information and strive to overcome the effects of the past. For them, there was always a sense of something not quite being right but never really being able to figure out what it was, or why life wasn't working for them. It is a relief to realize the problems can be fixed.

Drama stagers however, are well aware of their behavior and they coldly calculate using it to gain an advantage at the expense of those around them. They may have grown up in an addicted family, they may have grown up in a healthy family. They may have an addiction issue, they may not. They may or may not have mental health issues. Whatever their background is, the defining characteristic of these people is that they choose to continue acting in destructive ways because of the benefits it provides them. They can be merciless, and have no problem sacrificing other people and what is important to them. These folks have an inflexible narrative about themselves and the world. They will do anything to preserve, protect, and defend that narrative. They constantly scan for threats, challenges, or violations of their narrative.

Essentially, they have decided what their life should be like and assigned the rest of us roles that support their desired objective. We are almost always unaware of our role, but still get punished when we don't play our part. For example, someone may have a narrative that they are superior to everyone else. The role they have assigned themselves is to be the everlasting, brilliant star of any situation. The role they have assigned the rest of us is to be subservient. All of this goes largely undetected except for the uneasy gut feeling people get when they are around the drama stager. Until one day in a meeting, someone asks a question because they are seeking information, and the drama stager flips out because they think the person who asked the question is trying to make them look stupid. So they viciously verbally attack the person who asked the question. In their mind, the attack was justified because their rules were violated. But everyone else is horrified, and sees the attack as being wildly out of line. It is as crazy and convoluted as it sounds. It doesn't take more than one or two of these types of episodes before healthy people conclude something is really wrong with this type of individual, and start steering clear of them.

If you have more than one drama stager in the work environment, and their narratives serve one another's purposes, then you'll see even bigger and more chaotic scenes play out. In order to keep the drama going and keep everyone in an uproar so the focus is deflected from their own bad behavior, drama stagers attack people not problems. A lot of healthy people make the mistake of thinking that if they just solve whatever the drama stager is screaming about it will fix things and then there will be no more drama. But unfortunately that is a common scenario in which the drama stager exploits the healthy person's kindness or other values. Drama stagers don't want things to be fixed. They want their narrative to be reinforced. Spinning people in circles is the point. Actually fixing things is not. Drama stagers are weapons of mass disruption in the work environment, creating upheaval where there had been none before. These people use work to feed their own emotional needs, which bizarrely includes destroying people, places, and things. Work is a theater for them, a stage upon which their daily moods and whims can be acted out. Actually earning their paycheck and being a productive member of the work society is the furthest thing from their mind.

5. **Immaturity**. The last chapter started our conversation about this, but it is so vitally important that it must be included again in this list. As we talked about before, we all know people who simply have not grown up. Perhaps they are lacking in skills, or perhaps it is their choice. Regardless of the reason, they cause plenty of chaos in the workplace because they do not handle themselves in a mature, professional manner. There are lots of behavioral variations on this theme, but the core similarity is that these people are stuck at a developmental age very different from their chronological age.

These are the types of people who ridicule others. They bolster their own egos by making fun of pretty much everybody. They can be easily spotted, huddled up in the back of the room whenever a meeting is going on, laughing, poking each other, making faces, and otherwise showing off for each other. They can also be found in the lunchroom, gossiping, talking trash, and bullying their co-workers. I call this the arm-fart stage of development. It is behavior that is typically found at the junior high level. What these self-appointed cool kids fail to realize is that their behavior is transparent. They are acting big and trying to make others feel small to cover up their own insecurities. Healthy people see that, and find arm-farts during grown-up business meetings to be pathetic rather than funny.

Immature people also throw temper tantrums. Their emotional management skills are at a toddler's level of development. They routinely flip out over the most trivial matters. They become furious when larger problems arise, often lashing out at those who brought the issue to their attention. They are easily angered, and rage without constraint. This shows up as verbal abuse of others, slamming doors, throwing things, or a hundred other variations of childish behavior.

Immature people can also have adolescent style fits of rebelling and defying normal workplace protocols. Employees who are fixated on sexuality in an adolescent way are one example. They are the folks whose language is highly sexual in nature, and who twist just about anything that is said into having a sexual meaning. Another example is the employees who are deliberately loud and disruptive to their co-workers. They may refuse work assignments, slack off, whine, make excuses, and socialize rather than work. They take long breaks and lunches and expect everyone else to carry the load. They see work only as a paycheck, and are interested in doing the bare minimum necessary to keep it going. They treat professional workplaces like they are still at their first job at a fast food joint.

In addition to the five major issues described above, there are two other areas that can really trip us up personally and professionally: family of origin issues, and relationship problems. Even if you have excavated your own issues and worked them through to a good resolution, other people can keep you mired in problems that are not of your own making. If you are dealing with someone who has one of the five major impairments listed above, it will have an impact on you. It's essential that for your own well-being and the good of your team, you find ways to put good boundary lines around the problem.

Family of origin issues can follow us right into adulthood. Unhealthy families are unable to let go of control over their members. They demand that people remain in their old roles, following old rules. If anyone deviates from that script, it is considered a betrayal and punishment swiftly follows. Families of this type are especially outraged when people grow beyond the dysfunction and get healthy. Concerted efforts are usually made to get those who have wandered from the family narrative, to resubmit to family control. It isn't just parents either. Sometimes, parents are highly supportive of their adult children, but it is the siblings who want to keep the old family ways going because they get something out of it. It is absolutely ok to love these people anyway. But it is absolutely not ok to allow them to rob you of any aspect of your health, your relationship, or your career. If you can have a conversation to ask for the changes you need, have it. But if you think it won't be received well, or respected, then it falls to you to either limit contact with these people, or limit the impact they have on you and your life. Don't compromise your values or well-being for them. Hold that line. Enjoy the parts of the relationship that are good, if there are any. And either head home or take a break if things get to be too much. Make a decision in advance how you're going to respond (not react) when old stuff starts up. Then stick with your plan and make adjustments as time goes on. When you refuse to yield the healthy ground you have fought for and won for yourself and your life, other people will be forced to change how they relate to you. You might not ever change who they are, how they act, or what is wrong with them, but you will change how they relate to you and sometimes, that's enough.

Relationships, especially marriage, are an entirely different story. The person with whom you share your life has more of an impact on you than anyone. Your future is intertwined with them. This relationship deserves special care, and an investment of your time, effort, and energy. Getting this relationship right is one of the best gifts you can ever give yourself. Your personal and professional life can quite literally depend on it. Setting boundaries with them is essential too, but it is extraordinarily difficult not to be heavily impacted by what they choose to do. But it remains true that the healthier you are, the healthier the relationship becomes. Just like with your family of origin, it is absolutely not ok to allow them to rob you of your health or well-being in any area of your life.

There are four key areas that are foundational to building a successful relationship:

1) You. If you do not make healthy choices about how you live or relate, your relationship cannot be healthy.
2) Your partner. How well are you tending to, watching over, and supporting this one special person with whom you share your world?
3) The relationship. It is a living, breathing entity all its own. It is bigger than just the two of you, and it has a major ripple impact on those around you.
4) Navigating life together. Even if both of you are healthy, connected, and making your relationship a priority, life events will still happen and can throw things off track.

There are three main sources of stress that can drive any relationship to the breaking point:

1) Internal pressure generated by problems within one or both individuals. Dysfunctions that either one of you have automatically place great stress on the relationship.
2) Internal pressure that builds up within the relationship itself. Even if both of you are reasonably healthy within yourselves, but you relate to each other in a dysfunctional way, that also causes major stress in the relationship.
3) External pressure. This covers a full range of issues including job stress, other people meddling in your relationship, financial problems, and serious illness, to name just a few.

Starting with yourself is the right place to begin in building or fixing your relationship. It doesn't mean you have to take blame for things that aren't your fault, or that you have to excuse bad behavior. It does mean that you honestly take a look at yourself and make sure your own choices are healthy. If you have areas that you need to improve, that's ok. All you need to do is make the decision and get started. When you invest in yourself and strive to live to the best of your ability, there will be nothing holding you back from offering your best self to a partner. When both individuals are doing their best, they have an uncompromised opportunity to create the relationship of their dreams.

When you are in a relationship, your partner's life must become as important to you as your own. Your partner is not there to serve you or to save you, they are there to *share* life with you. Is your relationship faltering because you're not paying enough attention to them, or what's important to them? You don't expect to run a car without gas. You don't expect to manage a bank account without money. Attention and affection are the fuel and the currency of your life together. You can't have a successful relationship without them. Enjoy taking the time to get to know your partner in some new and important ways. Think about your partner's positive traits, and what they do well. Form an integrated perspective about your partner, one that honors the good, recognizes the flawed, and includes a lot of hope for the power of the human spirit to grow and improve.

Your relationship is as unique as a fingerprint. It is a living, breathing entity all its own. When you treat it as a sacred treasure, you maximize your chances of success. The examples of loving relationships we've seen in our lives greatly impact how we view relationships in general, and how we act in specific situations. The good news is that we can make healthier choices about how we define relationships and how we practice loving within them.

There are a lot of great relationship books out there, with many fine ideas about how to get along in general. But they fail to ask the one question that will make or break your relationship: ***how can you be successful with _this partner_.*** What each of us needs and wants in a relationship is as individual as we are. If we are listening, our partner is telling us how to be successful with them. When we pay attention and honor them, we have successful interactions. When we don't, we have trouble. If our partner is making a reasonable request of us, based on healthy needs, then there probably isn't a healthy reason for opposing or defying that request. Perhaps the details will need to be negotiated, but the request itself is not objectionable. You don't have to improve everything all at once. If you're overwhelmed, start with one thing, work on it, and then move on to the next. When you make a significant change, your partner will notice right away. One good change on your part tends to elicit one good change from your partner. Once this healthy cycle begins, momentum builds, problems get genuinely resolved, and pretty soon there is a brand new excitement and happiness in the relationship again.

Even the strongest couples can be stressed to a breaking point if the events in their life overwhelm their coping resources. Work to build up your ability to weather any storm that comes. Learning how to provide for and protect the relationship are vital tasks for building a lifetime of success together. A major part of having a successful relationship is having the ability and the willingness to negotiate how to handle whatever life brings your way, then honoring those agreements. When you provide for and invest in your life together, you stockpile resources that can be used when life gets rough. When you put protections in place, you create a buffer zone around the relationship to help it withstand anything that arises. The two of you can find shelter and stay strongly connected inside that buffer zone.

The Story of Ichabod

One day Ichabod had a new boss. Charlie's arrival was unexpected, but Ichabod figured he would be able to control their relationship the way he always had with so many others. But Charlie was a man who had done his work. He was in recovery, and knew nonsense when he saw it. He saw Ichabod as a small man who needed to continually puff himself up to bolster his fragile ego. He knew about Ichabod's family history, and the trouble he was in with the company. He refused to tolerate or negotiate the bad behavior. Ichabod was furious, but had run out of options. He hadn't taken previous incidents or attempts to reach him seriously, so finally being held accountable was a real shock to his system. He demanded a transfer but that was quickly declined. Ichabod was widely regarding as a liability, and no one wanted him anywhere near them. Ichabod thought he would just do what he had always done, which was settle into his anger, rally his troops, and target Charlie. But Charlie was different. He didn't cower in the face of Ichabod's bullying, nor did he lash out against it. He quite calmly advised Ichabod that he was putting him on a behavioral plan. Ichabod went nuclear in his attempt to get Charlie to back down. Charlie laid it on the line for him, explaining that Ichabod had been behaving badly for years and everyone before him had done him a disservice by letting him get away with it. Charlie told Ichabod he cared about him and the team too much to let him carry on with the same failed strategies. He outlined a behavioral plan for Ichabod that spelled out what would be acceptable and what would not be tolerated. He advised him that violations of the plan would result in a write-up, and after three write-ups, Ichabod would be terminated. Ichabod was stunned. No one had ever dared speak to him like this before. But there was something in Charlie's demeanor that let him know he meant business. Ichabod was faced with a choice. Grow up, or get out. His co-workers were massively relieved to finally see Ichabod face the consequences of his actions, and know that he wouldn't be allowed to torment them any longer.

The Story of Emma

Emma was a big fan of her local library. She checked out a wide variety of motivational and business speakers on CD. She listened to them in her car during her commute. Not all of the CDs were the best, but she usually learned at least something from each one. As she listened, she thought about two things: how the new information could help her as a person, and how it could improve her team. They were never far from her mind, and she loved them like her own family. They inspired her to become the best possible version of herself. One of the speakers taught powerfully about the impact families of origin have on our adult lives. She realized that while she had faced down her own demons, the addiction that plagued her family was still alive and well. She understood that she had more work to do in this area. She had made huge progress breaking the habits that kids who grow up in addicted families develop. What she still struggled with were episodes of family members causing total chaos when they were under the influence. Thankfully, she had a great marriage and her husband was very supportive of her efforts to grow. He knew that whenever she made a healthy change, it gave her more peace, and benefitted him and her team. They came up with a plan to deal with incidents of active addiction that crept into their lives. He and Emma were both very relieved to be setting some boundaries to contain the impact her family's addiction had on them.

Exercises

- ✓ Are you currently struggling with any of the five major impairments?
    - o Addiction: Yes / No
    - o Mental illness: Yes / No
    - o Criminal activity: Yes / No
    - o Drama stager: Yes / No
    - o Immaturity: Yes / No

✓ If you are struggling with any of those impairments, what are you going to do to address it:

_____

_____

_____

_____

_____

✓ Are you currently dealing with any issues in your family of origin? Yes / No
   o If yes, what are you going to do to address it?

_____

_____

_____

_____

_____

✓ Are you currently having problems in your relationship or marriage? Yes / No
   o If yes, what are you going to do to address it?

_____

_____

_____

_____

✓ What kind of self-development program would be appealing to you?

_____

_____

_____

_____

Chapter Three: Sustainable Life Practices

Setting a sustainable pace is a critical part of building a successful life. Being out of balance only works for so long. If you lose your health or your family along the way, it defeats the purpose. Your body, mind, spirit, and family must be able to tolerate what you are doing long-term. You are a vessel, and you want to have a clean, healthy flow. You do not want to be a clogged pipe filled with sludge. You have an enormous say in how long you live, and what the quality of that life is. Decluttering your life doesn't actually give you less, it gives you more. As you let go of obligations, attachments, habits, and possessions that serve no real purpose in getting you to your goal, your life becomes filled with only what is the most meaningful to you. You get to decide what your life is about.

The effort and energy required to reach your goals will vary over time. But keep in mind, that no endeavor in life requires nonstop maximum effort. The human body, mind, and spirit simply cannot sustain an endless level of high speed performance. We need to spend time planning when we need to work our hardest, balanced with the other things that matter the most to us in our life. Otherwise, people get exhausted. Operating from an exhausted state creates dangers we otherwise wouldn't face. Our thinking isn't as clear, and our decision making abilities are compromised.

Give yourself the gift of a carefully balanced strategy, and then trust your plan enough to follow it. Time, logistics, and finances may all need to shift. But if you've done an intentional, mindful job of thinking things all the way through, you'll have come up with a plan to minimize any negative impact. This is when self-discipline becomes a defining characteristic of your life. Some folks never come up with a plan to achieve their goals. Even fewer have a plan and do what it takes to get started. Even less get underway and stick with it when it gets hard. That means the self-disciplined person's chances of success are outstanding. It's going to take discipline to follow your plan. Remember though, that breaks are absolutely necessary when you need them. The beauty of a sustainable pace is that it has enduring flexibility that allows you to work hard then rest, while maintaining focus and building progress over the long-term. Once you have sustainable life practices in place, you will gain momentum that will carry you along.

One crucial area to be exceedingly mindful of is how you invest your energy. There is only so much of you to go around. Don't overcommit and don't allow dysfunctional people or situations to drain you of the energy you need to carefully protect for your most important priorities. Make sure you conserve your energy by taking time out from all the hard work and have some fun. Go to a ballgame, take the kids to the park, play with the dogs, surprise your spouse with a candlelight dinner, or whatever else will rejuvenate you and build the most important relationships in your life. Remember a huge reason you are doing this is because of them. If they are supporting your dreams, if your spouse is gracious enough to back you, and your kids and friends are cheering you on, then you owe it to them to be self-disciplined enough to build in break times with them. You want to look back and say you did right by people while you were accomplishing your goals. You want your support people to feel as good about the process you followed as they do about the finished product. Taking time to refresh yourself will be of great benefit to your team as well. The more rested and happier you are, the more of your best self you can bring to them.

You also don't want to ruin your own health. Some of us with Type-A personalities have to learn this lesson the hard way. Sometimes it takes a serious health scare to get our attention and show us the wisdom of a more sane pace of living. The human body was made for cycles of rest, work, and play. It was not designed for non-stop effort. Chronically pushing it beyond the pace of what your particular body can tolerate spells disaster. Eat well, exercise, and get enough sleep to feel rested. If your dream requires you to put in extra-long hours for a period of time, that's fine. But take a break when you need to and know when to get back to a more normal routine. You want to be alive and well to enjoy the fruits of your labors.

One essential way to conserve energy is to ignore distractions. You don't have time anymore for other people's pettiness or squabbles. If you've been involved in drama, exit stage left on the run! Nothing will throw a person off course quicker than drama. Some people lose endless amounts of time because they are entangled in problems that aren't even their own. Unless it involves a beloved friend or family member and your direct involvement is absolutely necessary, let people fight their own battles. We do bear a responsibility to protect our loved ones. However, if the person's crisis is self-generated and there's no real danger involved, it may be best to just stay out of it. Some people will never learn to make better choices until they begin experiencing their own consequences. We actually do them more harm than good by bailing them out of their endless scrapes. It is not your job to fix other people's lives, it is your job to fulfill your destiny. Just like you can't do other people's exercise routines for them, you also can't do other people's emotional or spiritual work for them either.

Another major energy drain is general negativity. You don't need to hear all that's wrong in the world right now. You need to be thinking about the positive. Better yet, this can be a vibrant time of celebrating all that is going well in your world. You can't afford to have someone put doubts in your head, tell you that you're crazy, or try to subtly convince you that you're in the wrong for even trying. Attitudes are contagious and you want to make sure you aren't unintentionally adopting anyone else's discontented worldview. You've carefully crafted your thinking and approach to your dreams, so guard that well, by not hanging around negative people or situations and absorbing their unhappiness. A few people enjoy the attention that stirring up trouble brings them, but they don't realize that their reputation spirals further downwards with every incident that takes place. Others love to gossip, and live for the wagging of their own tongue. You can end up in the middle of a mess before you know it. Don't take this particular form of manipulative bait, or fall into the trap like prey.

There is one other critical element of setting a sustainable pace we need to consider. Setting reasonable expectations for ourselves regarding how quickly we'll achieve our goals can prevent a lot of unnecessary mental strain. We need to take the long range view and focus on steady forward progress rather than overnight success. We can do everything else totally right but if we mess up in the area of setting expectations, we'll end up demoralizing ourselves. We can have the best attitude, support, and plan, but if we crush ourselves under the relentless pressure to succeed immediately, we'll end up quitting. If we quit, we guarantee our failure. Don't stress yourself out unnecessarily. You'll perform at your best when you take the excessive pressure off. The only truly sustainable pace is measured and relaxed. So if you are methodically putting in your best good faith effort, that's enough.

That goes for your team as well. Setting a sustainable pace will make or break your team. People's lives today can be highly stressful. You not only want to ease that stress because it's the humane thing to do, you also want to protect everyone involved by not pushing people to their breaking point. We all have one. Your job is to monitor your people's stress level and help them keep it in check. Don't push people so hard that their health, emotional equilibrium, or family life breaks down. You can't expect 100% effort from 100% of your people 100% of the time. Some days, someone showing up and doing the basic job may max out what they're capable of. Other days~ lots of other days ~ they'll be solid performers and sometimes superstars. You have to give them the breathing room to have fluctuations in their performance. They are only human.

Spend time getting to know your people well enough to know when they are off kilter. Talk with them and encourage them. Offer them information on community resources if they are struggling with issues outside of work. Some people face personal situations so daunting they need a little extra help to get through it. It's your job as a leader to balance accountability with compassion, and care about people on a human level. Helping them find outside assistance can resolve any workplace issues that might have cropped up, especially if you suspect that one of the major issues we discussed before might be impacting their work performance.

The Story of Ichabod

As had been his way all his life, Ichabod chose not to learn from his mistakes or the warnings of others. He seethed with rage at Charlie, not missing an opportunity to demonstrate anger towards him. What he was oblivious about was that Charlie was at total peace with the situation. Charlie knew he was doing the right thing by holding Ichabod accountable. He knew that Ichabod had been abusing his team for years, lying, cheating, and stealing from the company. He knew that Ichabod was a toxic presence on the staff. He understood that he was actually doing Ichabod a great favor by setting limits and offering him a chance to change. While Ichabod thought that his anger was getting to Charlie, that he was proving some kind of a point, he didn't realize that Charlie was completely calm in body, mind, and soul. He didn't dwell on what Ichabod was or wasn't doing. He monitored the behavioral plan in the necessary ways, but spent the rest of his time enjoying his job and focusing on the team as a whole. Ichabod's anger had no real impact on Charlie.

It was a completely different story however, inside Ichabod. He wasn't self-aware enough to listen to the warning signals from his own body. During his fits of anger he would have chest pains. His veins would bulge, his heart would race, and his blood pressure would spike. His mind was extremely agitated. His soul, which he was barely acquainted with at all, was in pain. He didn't realize that everytime he lashed out at Charlie, he wasn't hurting Charlie at all. He was only hurting himself. Every outburst took a greater toll. The stress hormones coursed through his body, his brain was firing like an electrical storm, and his heart was seizing up. But being convinced of his own omnipotence, Ichabod remained unaware of all this. As his body hurtled towards a health crisis, he also didn't comprehend that with every incident, he was handing Charlie all the evidence he needed to get rid of him.

The boiling point came at the first staff meeting after Charlie placed Ichabod on his behavioral plan. Ichabod did as he had always done, and started making faces at his buddies from across the room. They began talking loudly and disrupting the meeting. Charlie respectfully asked them to quiet down so that everyone could hear. Wanting to show off for his pals, Ichabod began challenging Charlie on pretty much everything he said. Charlie handled the interruptions well, and the staff was amazed at how calmly Charlie dealt with Ichabod. Many of them had an increasing level of anxiety, which Charlie could readily see. Ichabod continued carrying on with his nonsense, either not noticing or not caring about the frustration he was causing the team. He thought he was acting big and tough, but everyone except his few buddies saw him as weak, small, and pathetic. Charlie stayed the course and didn't waver. Ichabod had never experienced this before. He was used to upsetting the speaker, and getting his way. He normally disrupted meetings so much that they ended early. But Charlie kept everyone there the whole hour, and covered the entire agenda, even leaving time at the end for questions. Which people actually began to ask, once they realized that Charlie was going to keep control of the room and not let Ichabod interrupt or demean people. Within minutes the tide had turned and Ichabod and his buddies found themselves in the minority. The staff began to talk freely, and with each time Charlie shushed him, Ichabod's face grew redder and redder. He began to talk in a high pitched, whiny voice that trembled with anger. Even his pals sensed the change and backed off on their nonsense, leaving Ichabod alone with his antics. He became incensed at this perceived betrayal, never having realized that his pals were just using him because they thought he held some kind of special power. Once they realized that someone other than Ichabod held the true power, they abandoned him.

Charlie concluded the meeting and thanked everyone for their time. Then he asked Ichabod to meet him in his office. Ichabod was primed for a fight. He was confused and shaken at what had just happened. But his arrogance would not allow him to apologize and mend his ways. Instead, he barely made it into Charlie's office before he absolutely exploded. He began yelling and screaming obscenities at Charlie, who as always remained calm. Charlie pulled out the paperwork for Ichabod's first write-up. He had already filled it out, and took only a moment to add the day's events to the list of behavioral infractions. He reminded Ichabod that any further infractions would result in another write-up, and after the third one he would be terminated.

Ichabod's head was reeling. This had never happened to him before. He had always been able to talk or intimidate his way out of any situation he was in. Ichabod stormed out of the office, his face contorted into a mask of rage. He'd figure out a way to get that Charlie. He wouldn't allow him to do this to him. He stormed out to his car and peeled out in a blaze of screech marks and burning rubber. He hit the highway and accelerated well beyond the speed limit. He was screaming at the other drivers and weaving in and out of traffic. He had himself so worked up that he didn't notice the chest pains this time until it was too late. A massive heart attack rippled through his body. He lived just long enough to be conscious of slamming into the concrete barrier.

When Ichabod got to heaven, his entry was delayed. He was confused, and frightened. He didn't know where he was or why he was there. He saw person after person singing praises as they passed him and entered the pearly gates without hesitation. These people seemed ridiculously happy. Ichabod couldn't understand, and couldn't seem to make any progress towards the gates. He seemed rooted in place. After some time passed, an angel appeared and took Ichabod aside. He showed him a review of his entire life. For the first time, Ichabod had to face all the pain he had caused. At first he protested, and bellowed "why didn't anyone tell me it would be like this?!" To which the angel replied "we tried, but you wouldn't listen." The angel showed Ichabod all the moments in which people had tried to help him. Family, friends, ex-wife, his girlfriend, his boss, his team. "You were warned again and again to take things seriously and grow up" the angel said, "but you didn't listen."

The angel showed Ichabod the love people had once had for him, and how he had repaid their caring with pain. Shame and regret washed over Ichabod as he witnessed moment after moment of the heartache he had caused others. It made no sense to him now, why he had chosen to be such a jerk. He saw now that others still suffered, because of what he had done to them. He thought about his buddies, and how he had taught them it was cool for them to be jerks too. He realized that the ripple impact he had on the world had been incredibly negative. He suddenly understood that he had held great power in his hands, but squandered it in pursuit of selfish pleasures. As he faced an accounting of every instance of harm he had ever caused, Ichabod wept. He was a broken man. He was terrified about what would happen to him next. He had always bragged about knowing he was going to hell, but it wasn't funny any longer. The angel clicked off the film projector and asked Ichabod to explain himself. There wasn't even one single intelligent reply he could make. Instead, Ichabod began begging for a second chance. The angel was unimpressed, and sentenced him to a restless, anguished wandering just outside the gates.

The Story of Emma

One of the happy results of Emma's focus on self-development, was that she had acquired a lot of wisdom over time. When the children were still small, she and her husband sat down to figure out their priorities. They created a strategy for how they would balance their careers and family life, and they stuck with that through the years. At times it needed to be adjusted, but they always honored the spirit of their agreement that they would never let their jobs rob them of their health or make them a stranger to their children. Once the children were old enough, they taught sustainable life practices to them. They didn't let them overcommit in school or extracurricular activities. They modeled what they taught by carefully choosing what they invested their time, money, and energy into. Everyone in the family had a few cherished activities they got to participate in regularly. As a family, they resisted unnecessary distractions or disruptions to their lives. Everyone in the family also took time each day for their health and well-being. This was a must in their household. As the years passed, Emma was more and more grateful for the way of life she practiced. It brought her peace, comfort, and good health. It allowed her to thrive in her career, and take outstanding care of her team. She was so glad that she and her husband had agreed that not all promotions were worth it. They carefully vetted every opportunity that came their way, and never took a job that would require sacrificing their health or family life. Their life had certainly held its share of difficulties, but the foundation they had built was so strong that they weathered the storms unusually well. As she began to approach retirement, she was humbled and pleased to think about the difference she had made in people's lives. Her children were thriving in their adult lives. Her marriage was rock solid. Her life was filled with meaning. Her teams had gone on to great achievements, in no small part because of the confidence and skills she had given them. She had contributed significantly to several major company goals. It had been a great run, and Emma was happy with her results. She looked forward to the next stage of her life, and the chance to set a new vision of what else she might accomplish in her later years.

Exercises

✓ Only you can define which life activities / obligations are essential to being who you are and how you want to live in the world. Explain what is most important to you to keep.

_____

_____

_____

_____

_____

_____

_____

✓ List current drains on your energy or time, and ways you can recalibrate or let go of those situations so they don't compromise your well-being. Remember that sometimes, saying no to others really means saying yes to ourselves and the life we most want. Find ways to say no that excuse you from things you don't want to be involved in, while still preserving the relationships that you value.

_____

_____

_____

_____

_____

_____

✓ Describe the sustainable life practices you want to cultivate.

_____

_____

_____

_____

_____

_____

Part Two: Leadership of the Team

Teams are awesome! One of life's greatest experiences is working synergistically with a group of people towards a common goal for the greater good. Exponential results become not just possible, but probable when everyone is driven by the same vision. Taking a quantum leap forward together is an amazing experience. If you have never known the sheer joy of leading a team to victory you are missing out.

Teams can bring out the very best is a person, inspiring them to dig deeper within themselves to succeed than they would ever have the strength to achieve on their own. As a leader, you bear a sacred responsibility and privilege to get your part of the equation right. You owe the team your very best. As we learned in section one of the book, having your own self in order is the bedrock upon which your leadership will be built. If you're dysfunctional yourself, you will never see the dysfunction of people or situations in the work environment, and you will be an unmitigated disaster. There is no such thing as neutral leadership. You are either good enough, or you are having an adverse impact. The perils of abdicating responsibility are almost as bad as the perils of mistreating the team. If you are parked on your butt refusing to listen to issues, make decisions, or be proactive in creating a great environment for your team, you will quickly earn people's contempt. One of the most ridiculous phrases a leader can ever utter is "if you don't do anything about it, the problem will take care of itself." No! The problem will most assuredly *not* take care of itself. In fact it will get worse. Much worse, until one day it blows up in your face. In the meantime, people will accurately see you as weak, spineless, and a whole lot of other adjectives that aren't fit for print. Resentment towards you will grow until you are viewed with total scorn. You'll also be taken advantage of by those under your command who will sniff out and exploit your weakness every chance they get. Your life will become a dizzying merry-go-round from which you cannot escape. If you think being neutral is the answer, you really need to grow a set and get with the program.

After getting yourself squared away, the next item on the agenda is to learn how to properly treat a team. If you're still nursing a "me first" mentality, think of it like this: your life is much easier and your outcomes are much better when you treat people right. Here is the utterly sobering power of leadership: you literally hold your team's well-being and their quality of life in your hands. You have a massive ripple impact on their family and every community of which they are a part. Your reputation accompanies them everywhere they go. They can and do talk about you. Whether what they have to say is positive or negative is entirely within your control. If you're a jerk, that gets reported far and wide. If families incur medical bills because you're so much of a jerk that people get sick from the stress, your name appears in medical records as the cause. If marriages are being damaged, kids are being abused, or the family dog is getting kicked because you have driven someone beyond their breaking point, it will be all over social media. If you're unstable, or a drunk, or corrupt, or a thousand other variations of dysfunctional, that's getting shared like wildfire. One grave mistake bad leaders make is that they don't look beyond the narrow boundaries of their own system. They think they are in control because they are not yet fully facing the consequences of their actions. They're not bright enough or savvy enough to realize that the entire time they are behaving with impunity, there is a large and growing groundswell of disapproval and opposition that will one day knock them off their self-appointed pedestal and out of power.

Losing your reputation within the larger community will limit your future opportunities because word of your misdeeds will have preceded you. But it is not the only backlash you will face. Your current reality will erode out from under you like quicksand. People will stop trying to work with you. You'll miss out on important information and then situations you would have had an early warning about will erupt in your face one day. People will smile and nod but then quietly seek ways to correct whatever problems you are causing or allowing (or both). You will give people a common enemy to coalesce around. Productivity will shift from the mission of the organization to the goal of bringing you to justice. You can only mess with people for so long before they give up on you and fight back. Mess with the wrong person, who is better connected than you, healthier than you, or has more stamina than you, and you'll find yourself in a world of hurt in a hurry. Mess with someone's family, and the gloves will come off entirely.

You may be wallowing in denial and seeking allies wherever and however you can find them, but the fact is, the team sees the truth about you. Treat them badly enough, and they will join forces on a quest to put a stop to the hurt you are causing. When that happens, you'll find yourself on the outside looking in. Even if you survive the controversy, your power will be forever diminished and you will never be fully trusted again. The damage you caused other people will finally be visited upon your own doorstep. When the suffering quite rightly switches from the team to you, misery becomes your new normal while everyone else will be celebrating your fall. Your team is talking about you, in their living rooms, around the Thanksgiving table, in church, while playing sports, everywhere they go. You can't stop it. Consequently someday when you need something, you may run headlong into a brick wall because one of the people you need cares about one of the people you've hurt. They've heard the stories about what a jerk you are, and they'll be more than happy to deny what you want, to create a little justice in the situation. That's your social reality as a leader. There is only one of two scenarios: people are either singing your praises and raising your social capital, or you are handing them the ammunition that will eventually bring your reign of stupidity to a screeching halt.

So leaders my leaders, how do we get this right? We are arriving at the crux of this book. Even if you're a marvelously functional and mature adult, who does a remarkable job for your organization and is an upstanding member of your community, but you do not know how to properly feed and care for a team, you'll create an epic failure for yourself. You'll impose completely unnecessary hardship on every member of your team. We get leadership right by becoming awesome. What does that mean? It can be broken down into 3 critical components: interpersonal excellence, strategically developing others, and the art of consequences. Strap it up, and read on.

<u>Chapter Four: Interpersonal Excellence</u>

Interpersonal excellence is about a lot more than communication. It's a state of mind, a condition of the heart, and an active choice. It starts with the heart. If your heart isn't right towards your people, they will know it and nothing else you do will be effective. Eventually, you will face rebellion and mutiny. How do you get your heart right towards your people? You care about them. You care about the quality of the work environment you are offering them. You care about helping them succeed in a meaningful way in your organization. You care about the impact you are having on them, and their families. Bottom line, you care!

You also have to get your mind right. Realize that you do not own your people. You are not God. Your people are yours only for a time. This job working under your command is but one chapter in their life. Appraise your role realistically: you are one boss in one job at one time in their life. Don't puff yourself up with a bloated ego that strangles your ability to see reality clearly. You are not the big draw. They show up to work every day because they need the money to take care of who or what they love in their life. They don't show up because you're so marvelous they just can't stand to be apart. Respect your people as individuals with inherent value that has nothing to do with you. Understand that they have goals and dreams and lives outside of work that are what their life is really all about. You provide the paycheck. Don't ever try to hold someone back, don't ever mistreat anyone, and don't ever mess with someone's life or family. Bottom line: have a mental attitude of respect.

Good leadership is an active choice. Awesome leadership takes total commitment. Anyone can suck at leadership, and many people do. Don't be the whiny tyrant who perches on their leadership chair and bellows about how magnificent they are. That reduces you to a caricature of yourself. A version of who you are that can be taken about as seriously as a cartoon. You have not ascended to some lofty station that makes you better than anyone else. You haven't arrived. You hold one position in one organization for one period of time. Your "leadership" might well be considered a joke in a different organization. The nonsense you are allowed to get away with at one place would get you fired at another. So before you coronate yourself ruler of the universe, remember that a vast legion of leaders has come before you, and even more will come after. This is just a moment in time, so it would be wise for you to keep the magnitude of your self-appointed grandeur in perspective. Make the choice to be a leader who serves rather than trying to force others to serve you. That one decision alone puts you on the path to greatness.

You also have to work on building trust with your people. Trust is the only currency that matters. If your people don't trust you, they won't talk to you. If they don't talk to you, you won't know what's really going on. A day will come when one of your people makes a mistake, or something bad happens, and you will need to know about it in real time. Your people will not come to you with the news unless you already took the time and made the effort to build trust with them. If they don't trust you, you will miss out on important knowledge that can massively blow up in your face later on. Set a goal to build trust with every interaction. This means really listening to your people, especially if they are upset. Don't take their upset personally. We all have different frustration tolerances and stress thresholds. Don't get offended, or insulted, or have a weak ego by being too fragile to listen to them. Don't retaliate. Hear them out. Work with them to discuss a solution. Don't try to hurry up and get the conversation over with, or cram your rigid opinion down their throat. They feel how they feel. They think what they think. It is absolutely your job as the leader to be the bigger person and demonstrate respect and caring. It is your job to model problem solving skills, especially under pressure. You're the one with the authority and the power to solve problems, so man up and get to it. Your team will be a reflection of you. Do you want them to learn great skills that make the workplace better for everyone, or poor skills that make any situation that arises even worse? Remember, your behavior sets the tone and then you get to live with the consequences of that. Why wouldn't you want good outcomes in every situation you face? You are responsible for being trustworthy, and for building trust with your team.

There is one more aspect to the importance of trust in the work environment. It is impossible to emphasize this point enough: maintain your objectivity. Some of the biggest scandals we've heard about on the news happened in no small part because a leader trusted someone they shouldn't have. Otherwise good leaders make the mistake of trusting without verifying. Don't be intellectually or emotionally lazy and fail to keep an open mind about what is really going on. Just because you worked with someone years ago doesn't mean you know them now. Just because they are slick talkers doesn't mean they are telling the truth. Blindly trusting anyone is asking to be lied to, manipulated, or exploited. If you hear yourself saying the words "They would never…" you know it's time to stop and think. What if the unpleasant information you're hearing is true? Reestablishing your emotional comfort at the expense of the truth makes you look like a weak idiot. You are putting your good name on the line when you back someone without ascertaining the facts for yourself. Depending on the situation, that could be a career ending move. And in today's litigious climate, you could also bear personal liability for not properly handling the situation.

As a leader you can make a tremendous impact the way no one else can. Bear this responsibility wisely. The joy of leadership is learning your people, what matters to them, what upsets them, what motivates them, what optimizes their abilities, and then guiding them accordingly. You should know the basics about every one of your direct reports. Yes, every one! Talk to them and learn what their personal and professional dreams are, and what their life outside the office is like. You're not looking to pry, you just want to know enough to understand where they are coming from, what struggles they may be facing, and what they hope to accomplish with their life as a whole. Then use this information to guide how you lead them as an individual. Each day you need to recalibrate expectations and interactions with each person. No one gives exactly the same level of performance 100% of the time. You will maximize each person's contribution to the organization when you help them deliver their best on any given day. If they're going through a rough time, show some mercy. If they're on fire with enthusiasm, give them the ball and let them run with it. Most days will be in between, so help them establish a steady baseline of performance that allows them to be and give their best.

It is your responsibility to help your people grow personally and professionally. You are there to serve them, they are not there to serve you. Together, all of you are in the service of the mission. If someone missed out on lifeskills as a kid, it's your job to help them develop in those areas. For example, if someone didn't learn how to handle their emotions well in childhood for whatever reason, it is your job now to help them learn how to handle them in the work environment. You need to care about the team and protect the environment by holding people accountable to acceptable standards of behavior. Don't make or accept excuses. Most people are capable of change. If they don't have organic issues interfering with their ability to understand and choose new behavior, then they will almost certainly be highly motivated to make the required adjustments in order to keep their job. You do a massive disservice to people when you allow bad behavior to continue. What is unacceptable now will only get worse as time goes on, and the consequences will grow more severe. When you allow someone to think acting up is ok because you don't correct it, you are harming that person's future. They will continue their bad behavior until one day it is out of control and someone else steps in to stop in. You'll be corrected at that point too, for letting the situation gain a foothold and flourish. Ultimately however, you are spiritually responsible for the years you delay or hinder someone's growth as a person when you allow bad behavior to go unchecked. You really don't want to reap that kind of a harvest.

Your goal is to treat people equitably, not equally. If someone is able to produce 20 widgets a day, and someone else is only able to produce 10, and your company's minimum per day is 10, then both of your workers are meeting the goal. If you try to force the 10 widget person to do 20 you will overwhelm them to the point of non-functioning. If you restrict the 20 widget person to only 10, you will offend and frustrate them to the point of demotivation. The point is to maximize the abilities of each person, while holding them accountable to minimally acceptable standards. Not everyone can be a superstar. There is no one size fits all approach to people. Every individual is unique. One of the most refreshing aspects of leadership is that it doesn't matter what has worked with anyone in the past. Each time you gain a new direct report, you have to start all over again and learn how to lead that particular person. That's why leadership is endlessly fascinating, and can never be truly mastered.

Your direct reports will represent a bell curve. At one tail end of the curve are the people who struggle. Your job will be to help them improve. It's up to you to figure out what is wrong and help them fix it. The solution will be dependent on that individual and their specific needs. Remember that the process of how you try to solve the problem is as important as the work you're trying to produce. People have to feel good about both, or your plan will fail. The majority of your people will rest under the apex of the bell curve. They will form the backbone of your team. They won't struggle, but they aren't superstars either. These folks need to be treated well with minimal intervention from you. Let them work. They are a self-motivated lot with a good work ethic and you can count on them for the long-haul. You rarely see behavior problems in this subset of people, they are simply too busy doing the job to be bothered with nonsense.

At the other tail end of the curve are the high performers. These people are a gem and need to be managed differently than any other group. They approach work as a collaborative venture. They take tremendous ownership of their job and their contribution to accomplishing the mission. They generally have a lot of executive level skills, although their actual position in the company may be at a different level. They will treat you more as a business partner than a traditional boss. Cherish that. They are your quintessential team players, who make up for the deficits of the low performers, help stabilize the middle of the pack, and attend to culture just as much as they do to results. They are thoughtful observers of people and processes. When they think something can be improved, they will let you know. Cherish that too. Their ability to speak truth to power is invaluable to you. They need you to support what they are trying to accomplish, and then they need you to get out of their way and let them shine. Don't ever suppress the talents of a high performer. Doing so would be like benching the star quarterback on a football team so that the backup doesn't feel bad. Do you want to win the game or not? Let people excel when, where, and how they can. You want to keep your high performers happy. Without these people, your personal results tank. Your middle-of-the pack performers will not be able to raise the low performer's results enough to prevent a lot of negative attention from being directed your way for failing to meet objectives.

A Tale of Two Managers

Emma

Emma loved her people, as individuals and as a team. She had a heart for giving them the best work life possible. She understood the role she played in their lives. She knew that she was just one aspect of their life, but that she held tremendous power in her hands to help or hurt them. She chose to help. She was a person of faith, and had long ago decided that her leadership would be about the example of Jesus washing his disciple's feet. Servant leadership was a guiding principle of the decisions she made. She truly enjoyed her team, and cared about their success both at work and outside of it. She was known for doing kind things for people, connecting them with resources they might not otherwise have access to, and recommending them for new opportunities. She authentically loved to see people succeed, and she never expected anything in return. More than one career had taken a giant leap forward because of her efforts.

She cared enough to get to know her team as people, not just as workers. She knew the hopes, dreams, and struggles of every person on her team. Over time she developed the ability to read each of them. She knew when someone was having a bad day and she showed a lot of compassion and mercy towards them. She knew when someone was pushing to meet a goal and was a steadfast supporter doing all she could to help get them there. She knew when to push, and when to back off. She knew when to confront and challenge, and when to defend and advocate for her people.

Every new person was immersed in the culture of the team. This group was different. They decided together what they wanted their work life to be like, and how they would meet organizational goals. Then they held each other accountable. It was a two way street. Emma was known for being calm and grounded. People would come to her upset and she would actually listen, then work with them to figure out a solution. She let them know when she didn't approve of something they had done, and they did the same with her. It was a commitment they had all made to each other in the beginning. They respected her greatly for this.

Emma expected each of her people to be who they were. Others might try to coach people to pose or posture, but never Emma. She insisted they be authentic. She worked to build trust every time someone came to see her. She encouraged people to speak their minds. She knew that festering emotions turned into undercurrents of discontent that would pull people under as surely as a rip tide at the beach. She had people of all abilities on her team. She worked with her low performers to bring them up to an acceptable level. She spoke candidly with them about figuring out what their best efforts were and how to produce those results consistently. She treasured her many solid performers, expressed tremendous gratitude to them, and then let them do their jobs.

She was close with her high performers. She used to be a high performer herself when she held a front line position, and she would always have a soft spot in her heart for the hard charging sorts who were passionate about making an impact. She leaned on this group, challenging them and demanding they become their very best. This group was hungry for growth, and she set goals with them that appeared to the individual to be just out of reach. Emma kept believing in them, exhorting them to stay the course, and as time passed they were amazed at all they could accomplish. Most of them went on to better opportunities, and would come back later and thank Emma for the influence she had on their lives. She was so proud of each of them, and genuinely thrilled about their success. She had known all along they were hers for only a time anyway, and that it was her job to help them take the next step towards their dreams and goals. It gave her great joy to know she fulfilled that responsibility well and helped people to become a little bit more of what God had called them to be.

Mrs Rogers

Mrs. Rogers was the anti-Emma. She was not a person of faith and in fact sneered at anything that resembled higher ordered thinking or living. She hated her people and actually told them so. Repeatedly. When people tried to talk to her she would cut them off and start spewing her opinion. She had very little emotional control and was highly reactive. She would rage at people without restraint, sometimes coming close to physically hitting them. She spoke with a nasty hissing tone, like a venomous snake intent on striking. She believed her team was there to serve her, and she put her emotional comfort above all else. She lived in such denial that even when things were falling apart right in front of her face, she refused to admit the truth. Her weaknesses were evident to everyone. Good people were repelled by her behavior. People with their own agendas exploited and used her. No one trusted her. She spent her day abusing people and her position. The mission of the organization was of no importance to her. Her mind was a poisoned cesspool of negativity and sludge. She enjoyed the damage she caused, and was intoxicated by the power she held in her hands. If someone needed a letter of recommendation, she would call and tell lies to ruin the opportunity. She coddled low performers, often exchanging special favors they would do for each other. She put enormous pressure on her middle-of-the-pack people, overloading their work schedules to the breaking point. She loathed her high performers and publicly ridiculed and opposed them. Her team was forced to attempt to meet goals in spite of her. She sowed seeds of division and disharmony every chance she got. She lied regularly and cut shady backroom deals to further insulate herself from consequences. A lot of good people left. Others decided to stay and fight, and she ultimately found herself embroiled in controversy that she could not extract herself from.

Exercises

For every one of your direct reports, write down the following:
- ✓ their career goal
- ✓ at least one non-career goal
- ✓ what their life outside the office is like
- ✓ what matters to them
- ✓ what upsets them, and
- ✓ what kind of rewards are meaningful to them

If you are unable to write down that info, then this is the perfect opportunity to get to know your team!

Chapter Five: Strategically Developing Others

By far, strategically developing others is the best part of leadership. You're not there just to help people meet goals like robots on an assembly line. You're there to help people *grow*. The best leaders I have ever known are passionate about helping people evolve to the next level. For me, it has always been one of my greatest professional joys to watch people grow into more of who God called them to be. In my professional world, it just really doesn't get any better than that.

You don't want some haphazard plan for helping people develop skills. You want to be strategic about it. Keep the main thing you are there for the main thing you focus on. Never compromise meeting goals and fulfilling the mission for developmental activities. Use skills building opportunities as a supplement to what people are already doing, in a way that's appropriate for each one of them. Match people's skills and needs with the organization's operational and cultural needs/gaps. This is a great way to shore up skills for those who are struggling, and is highly motivating for high performers. It also breaks up the monotony for middle-of-the-pack workers.

Make developmental activities a fun diversion from the norm for everyone. This is a wonderful way to help prepare people for promotion, or greater opportunities in their outside lives. It is a highly strategic way to position people for success. It is a win-win for everyone. The organization and the employee both benefit from enhanced skills that add value in real time and in the future. Help people build job specific competencies, plus generally useful skills like public speaking. Increasing people's value to the organization is always a smart choice. Create a plan in consultation with each individual. Find out what they are interested in learning. Challenge them with goals that stretch them as people. I've seen amazing results from this type of process. For example, if someone has great leadership potential but struggles with being shy, make overcoming that a goal. Give them opportunities to help you lead meetings with a small number of people. Then have them work in a group to deliver training to a small number of people. Then have them work in pairs to deliver training to a significantly larger group. Then finally, have them deliver training to a large group on their own. They will find a whole new level of confidence, and shyness will no longer hold them back from pursuing or landing new opportunities. Once your people experience success with this process, your team will be invested in continually improving.

You can have a lot of fun together setting, working towards, and attaining new goals in a variety of areas. You know you've gelled as a team when everyone is all-in and working towards the best possible results for themselves and each other. That's what it's really all about. Business, sports, academics, whatever sector you're in is just a vehicle for learning how to accomplish something great by working together with a team of people for the common good. This is one of life's most valuable lessons.

When you are seeking to develop others, leverage your power and connections for their good. If you have the ability to help someone get ahead, do it. Introduce people, set up mentoring relationships, assign staff to special projects together, and use your influence to open doors. Power was made to be used for good, not evil. For the sake of the whole, not for self-serving motives. Delegate power as much as you possibly can. Put people in charge of initiatives and events. Give them the chance to see what you do all day, or let them shadow someone else who does what they aspire to. Give people as much special responsibility as makes sense for them and for you, and then help them succeed in their new role.

One skill that is essential to help people build regardless of what arena your leadership is in, is stress resilience. Life moves at an increasingly fast pace with ever widening global implications. On a daily basis our brains are bombarded with information and our emotions have to navigate a maze of experiences that can leave us exhausted, frazzled, and worn out. Learning how to deal effectively with stress is a critical skill for all life stages. All of us have a frustration tolerance beyond which we cannot cope. We are having a lot more serious health problems at younger ages because our bodies just cannot keep up with the demands stress places on them. Stress resilience can be trained, and everyone benefits from learning it. You will have a good start down the road of building a healthy work culture if everyone is working on handling their own stress well.

Finally, strategically developing others sometimes means helping someone rehabilitate their career. It is your job to lead the way in assisting those who have messed up with regaining their equilibrium and restoring good relationships with the team. If termination is not possible or appropriate, then it falls to you to help make the situation right. You need to teach and practice forgiveness. Mercy is required. This is a non-negotiable aspect of a healthy environment. It doesn't mean you condone bad behavior or allow it to continue. It doesn't mean that everyone will like or trust each other. It does mean that once the offense has been dealt with, people don't hang onto it so they can move forward. If someone has really messed up and hurt the team, let people voice the impact the transgressions had on them. Making them stuff their thoughts and feelings will only serve to further entrench the problem. It's also part of taking full accountability for the offender to realize the impact of their behavior on other people. Quite frankly, the offended need to be heard, and the offender needs to hush up and listen and work to make things right with the team.

Don't settle for a fake peace. You're the leader, this is part of the job. Do the hard work necessary to help offenders mend fences. Do the hard work necessary to help the offended process and move past the problem. Your goal is a team who works professionally together. If someone has breached trust, it is going to take some time to build a new normal together, but it can be done. Reconciliation is possible for a manager with the backbone to face the issues head on and lead the team through the mess. There are a lot of incredibly valuable life lessons inherent in this process, and it will serve your team well in their professional and personal lives, for the rest of their life. We are only human. Mess ups are inevitable. Moving past them is often not done, and is rarely done well.

When you immerse yourself and your team in an environment of growth, it builds esprit de corps and momentum. People show up every day excited to be working on their goals, rather than dreading or resenting coming in. They are focused, and get their regular responsibilities taken care of so they can get to the fun stuff. Pretty soon they encourage, support, and correct each other as they pursue their goals, and when that happens, it is a thing of beauty. The best environments I have ever been a part of are all about doing the main job well, while aspiring to greater heights. Together.

A Tale of Two Managers Continued

Emma

Emma had a passion for helping people grow and learn new skills. She met with her people regularly to find out how they were really doing. She was adept at discerning people's strengths and developmental needs. She helped them chart a course for gaining the skills they needed and wanted to learn at that point in time. Everything was geared towards helping them grow as people and increase their value to the company, while positioning them to compete well for the next job they hoped to land. She also helped them understand how their skill set was viewed from a management and organizational perspective. Everyone was working on something, including Emma. She respected them enough to ask her team where they thought she could improve, and then she set about making those changes. Their days were filled with attending to their regular business, and then getting to the fun stuff, as they affectionately referred to their projects. There was very little squabbling among her staff. Each person felt valued and was given a meaningful way to contribute.

Mistakes, including Emma's, were dealt with compassionately in real time. They held each other accountable, and their staff meetings were very different from most other groups. Most organizational meetings were boring renditions of information that could have easily been conveyed in a simple e-mail. Not so with Emma. The team sat together as a group and talked about the real issues they were facing, in candid, colorful terms.

Respect was the one ground rule, and people were able to air, discuss, and resolve issues they were having with procedures or with each other. Each person was asked but not forced to participate. Some people had a lot to say, some just a little, but all of them knew they were welcome to say what was on their minds. Emma greatly valued these meetings because they did a lot to keep the team on track with each other, and they gave her important information about problems so she could help fix them. It also highlighted what was working well, and those things were easy to build upon. Other than private goals that people might prefer to keep to themselves, the team sat and talked about the progress they were making towards individual and group objectives. This was one of their primary tools for holding themselves and each other accountable.

When it was clear things weren't going well, Emma taught the group how to step back from the situation and view it from different perspectives. She always encouraged them to think about whether or not the root source of the problem was operational or interpersonal. Most of the time it was operational, even if it felt like it was interpersonal. She taught them how to take the long-range view, the big picture view, and the objective view. She encouraged them to walk in the door with a possible solution for each problem they brought up, or at least be able to say they had been thinking about possible solutions but hadn't come up with one yet. These discussions were robust, not always easy, and not always pleasant. But they had them. People showed each other a lot of empathy and mercy without accepting excuses. Together they came up with solutions to most of the problems they faced. They pledged support to each other and then followed through with whatever they said they would help with. Emma was a stickler for follow through, and the team had long ago adopted this way of thinking. Emma's role evolved into coach and referee, and she had a great time mentoring people as they learned how to be responsible for themselves and their teammates. She was still their undisputed leader, but what she had taught them became so ingrained, they needed very little active managing from her. Her team amassed an impressive array of tangible skills and were soon in demand as trainers for other departments, but she was even more pleased with the intangible skills that made them one of the best teams in the business. She was proud of them, and told them so.

Mrs. Rogers

Mrs. Rogers never bothered to take her own development seriously, so she never had any interest in it for anyone else. In fact, she mocked it. In her world, you got jobs not because of what you know but because of who you know. She had always strongarmed or sold herself out to get the next position. More pay and prestige was all she was after. Her people weren't even an afterthought, she simply didn't care about them at all. She viewed them as a nuisance to even have to deal with. She had no qualms about breaking their backs as she stepped on them to elevate herself one more rung up the ladder. She manufactured false images of people, peddled them to the unsuspecting, and then ferociously protected the narrative she had spun. She refused to let anyone under her make a new connection because it threatened the negative story she had already told. She didn't want anyone getting to know or like her people. She didn't want her lies to be exposed. She would scream about how she had to wait years to get where she was and she would not allow anyone to succeed faster or more easily than she had. She possessed an old school mentality that everyone should wait their turn in a long line before they were picked for a new opportunity. She was too ignorant and arrogant to realize that a lot of people thought very differently than she did. She would brutalize people in order to attempt to keep control over them. She was a miserable, cynical person who demanded that other people not be happy either. She would actually claim that she wanted people to suffer. She only called meetings to berate people for their perceived transgressions. She actively discouraged people from pursuing new opportunities, and if they did go after their goals anyway, she punished them. Her team was a seething cauldron of drama that broke out with regularity, and prevented the good workers from getting their own jobs done. The environment she created was toxic, and people did only the bare minimum to keep from getting fired.

Exercises

- ✓ For each of your direct reports
    - o Based on what you already know about them, sketch out a plan to help them accomplish their professional goals
    - o Talk to them about what specific skills they would like to work on
    - o Create a plan together to accomplish the chosen objectives

<u>Chapter Six: The Art of Consequences</u>

This defines a leader! You *must* be willing to administer consequences for people's bad behavior. If you're not, you need to do the honorable thing and step down. Immediately. Nothing demoralizes good workers or ruins cultures more quickly than not holding people accountable. Lazy or dysfunctional employees poison the well so that no good water flows from it. It is impossible to have an authentically healthy workplace when people are allowed to not produce, or to act in disruptive ways. Choices have consequences. Stop feeling sorry for the people who are facing consequences, and start feeling sorry for the person who would really appreciate the job and do it well. Nothing is more dangerous for the problem individual himself (or herself) than to be allowed to get away with unacceptable behavior. You have the opportunity to help someone gain control of themselves and succeed. If you don't exercise this responsibility, you are setting them up for a much harder fall sometime in the future. When you allow or encourage them to act up, you are feeding their dysfunction. You're also hurting the team you're tasked with protecting. If you are the reason the problem isn't being fixed, then ultimately you will be held accountable for it.

It's time to get in touch with your inner warrior and get real about solving problems. When you send the message that the environment will be healthy and productive, respect will reign. Your reputation as a weakling will vanish. Immature people will stop pushing the boundaries and grow up. Dysfunctional people will think twice before pulling the same old nonsense. They might even get help for their issues. And the good people will be dancing up and down the hallway because you *finally* cowboyed up and addressed the problems!

Your goal is deceptively simple: correct the behavior. If someone is being lazy, they need to work. If someone is volatile, they need to stop having outbursts. If someone is acting crazy, they need to get ahold of themselves. For every problem you face, at its core it's a simple one to resolve. Don't overcomplicate it. Sometimes people just plain need to knock off their foolishness. They are capable of acting better, and they would choose to act better if only you would make them. Barring organic or cognitive issues that prevent a person from fulling engaging with reality, most people know that their behavior is a problem. It's gotten them in trouble for a long time, but since no one ever says ENOUGH and holds them to it, they just continue on with the same old stagnant ways of dealing with the world. Your organization, your team, your own peace of mind, and the problem child themselves deserve better from you. You wouldn't allow a toddler throwing a temper tantrum to drive the company car or go negotiate a deal. Why are you letting emotional toddlers in adult bodies do just that? Banish the excuses and demand better. Have enough respect for the problem individual to require acceptable behavior. You know they can do better, and so do they. So make them.

The first thing you need to do is precisely determine the scope of the problem. Face the truth that trouble has been brewing for a long time and you've been ignoring, minimizing, or dismissing it. Low grade nonsense goes on everyday, and dysfunctional people use those instances as surveillance missions for what they can get away with. Don't ignore the rude remarks, the emotional volatility, the shirking of duties. You're being tested. Stop flunking the pop quiz and deal with things in real time. Dysfunctional people need to know their usual modus operandi won't work with you, and the good people need to see that you are protecting them and the sanctity of the work environment. And you gain a reputation as a problem solver instead of a wimp.

The next thing you need to do is mindfully consider alternative strategies for correcting the problem. Your goal is to fix the behavior, not crush the person. You can be firm and respectful. The fix needs to be fair and reasonable. It needs to directly relate to the problem, and it needs to require a new and better action on the offending person's part. Don't be ruled by your emotions, or your dislike of the person. Everyone deserves equitable treatment. If it was your best employee that pulled the same boneheaded move, how would you be handling it? Make sure that the focus remains on fixing the problem. And remember that if you abuse the corrective action process by going too far with it, then you become the problem and the consequences shift to you.

Once you've decided on what you believe will be the most effective course of action, the next step is to implement the solution. Sit the person down and explain exactly what you are doing, why you are doing it, and what is expected from this point forward. Dysfunctional people will try all sorts of things at this point to get you to back down. They will throw a temper tantrum, cry manipulative tears, deny ever having done anything wrong in their entire life, blame childhood circumstances for their misdeed, or claim the devil made them do it. Stay calm and strong. They use these methods because other people have given in to them their entire life. The drama stops with you. You are the one to stand up and demand and get better out of them, and in so doing, you are teaching them a more effective way to live. Hold your ground and let them know that whether they like it or not, whether they agree to it or not, whether they even acknowledge it or not, these are the consequences you are implementing effective immediately. Make it crystal clear for them that regardless of what they think or feel, they are responsible for following the new rules and will be held accountable to them. Then fully expect them to go right out and test them, to see whether you are serious about the solution or not.

Monitor their adherence to whatever you imposed on them. Good employees who run afoul of the rules will be mortified to have messed up and will police themselves so you don't have to. Dysfunctional people may decide that acting up just isn't worth the hassle anymore, and start making better choices. Or they may ratchet it up and try to escalate the situation to once again be to their liking (ie they are in control while you are sucking your thumb in your office wondering what to do). Hold the boundary line you set. Once they see that you mean business, and that their shenanigans will no longer be tolerated, if they have any capacity for self-control at all they'll knock it off. Those with genuine mental or psychological problems might not be able to control themselves, and will require active recalibration of the work environment as well as extensive coaching to try and fix the issues. But chances are these folks are not the ones causing all the drama anyway. Drama is usually instigated by people who to some degree choose it, not by people who struggle just to keep up with the demands of life.

The last key to effectively putting a stop to bad behavior, is that once you've implemented your plan and are monitoring compliance, it's time to get back to leading the rest of the team. This sends the problem person the strong and accurate message that when they act up they get a swift consequence and then life moves right on. Don't unwittingly allow someone to become a star in a protracted battle with you. Once you've handled the issues, give your attention right back to the team. There are no doubt plenty of ruffled feathers to smooth out there. Assure them you have dealt with the problem and won't allow it to recur. This is generally all they need to know in order to move past whatever happened. If it was a serious incident, then they deserve a candid conversation with you to talk about what took place. They also deserve resources for coping with the impact the incident had on them. It may be as simple as a private conversation inquiring if they are ok, or as intensive as a trauma response team brought in for people to talk with if they so choose.

A Tale of Two Managers Continued

Emma

Emma let her team know in the very beginning that doing their jobs and treating each other with respect was non-negotiable. Nearly everyone readily adhered to these ground rules. A few lazy or dysfunctional folks tested the limits but quickly learned that Emma would hold them accountable. They soon realized that it wasn't worth the hassle to keep getting in trouble and they brought their behavior in line with minimally acceptable standards. Emma and the team could live with that. People who were unwilling to change their behavior requested a transfer to another department. The manager they gravitated to was as lazy and dysfunctional as they were. Emma and her team were glad to be rid of them. Her team wasn't perfect, and they didn't all like each other with equal enthusiasm, but they did work well together as one cohesive whole. They'd been through good times and bad together, and they valued the working environment they had created. They could count on one another, and that was enough.

Emma had a reputation for not allowing nonsense on her team. Her people had bad days and difficulties in their life outside the office just like anyone else, but they handled them better than most. Emma was always on top of these dynamics, easing stress where she could, applying pressure when needed, and keeping everyone focused on that day's workload. It was a formula that had been highly effective for them.

Above all, Emma protected the team. She told everyone that if she ever had to make a choice between one individual and the team, she would choose the team, every single time. She refused to sacrifice the good of the many for the wishes of the one. A few people had been surprised because they thought their closeness with Emma would keep them out of trouble. Not so. When people committed serious violations, Emma held them accountable too. Consequences were meant to correct problems and protect the team. She was fair and reasonable in what she decided to do to fix bad behavior, and she monitored progress until she was thoroughly convinced that the problem had been overcome. Along the way she coached people about the importance of maintaining standards, and the impact it had on other people and their own future. She was always compassionate in these discussions. She never used correction as retaliation. She was able to forgive and move on better than most. This created an environment where people could admit mistakes and know they would be treated humanely while Emma helped them fix it. It facilitated a culture in which people didn't want to disappoint her by messing up, so they made extra efforts to do a good job. She had a way of bringing out the best in people and they respected her for it.

Mrs. Rogers

Mrs Rogers was vengeful by nature. She demanded people sacrifice themselves to protect her from her own consequences. People were commodities to her, nothing more. She enjoyed inflicting pain, and punishing people for a wide variety of things she felt were objectionable. She was moody and what pleased her one day infuriated her the next.

There was no consistency in how she acted or treated her team. She would tell her people that she couldn't stand dealing with them. They wouldn't have admitted a mistake to her if you paid them big money to do it. If a mistake did come to her attention, she would publicly humiliate the person and then spend hours relaying the gossip to her cronies in other departments. She had no internal moorings that helped her withstand the normal human problems of working together in groups. She had no plan for dealing with conflict. She was extremely reactive and made snap judgments based on incomplete or skewed information. She imposed harsh punishments that far exceeded what misdeed had been committed. She didn't think much at all about what she did, except to make sure it caused as much damage as possible. She sought to crush people, not correct behavior. She could turn anything into a personal affront. She abused the disciplinary process as a way to express her personal vendettas. Once someone offended her, she hated them forever, and nurtured that hate until it grew into a towering inferno of evil. Problems were driven underground and there was constant tension as people sought to steer clear of her insane behavior. Productivity was compromised and goals went unmet. Mrs Rogers was too foolish to see that the seeds she was sowing would one day grow into a harvest that would be her own undoing.

Exercises

You know who on your team needs to be have their behavior or productivity corrected. Come up with a plan to make that happen.

_____

_____

_____

_____

_____

_____

_____

_____

_____

_____

Part Three: Leadership of the Organization

In addition to leading yourself and your team, you are also responsible for leading the organization. You've been entrusted with serious responsibilities to help shepherd the group as a whole. You are one of a cadre of managers that should all be working towards the common good of the people, the mission, and the bottom line. It really doesn't matter if the bottom line is about profits, championships, or being a wise steward of taxpayer dollars. What matters is that you are part of a larger team of leaders working together to achieve those objectives. You don't operate in a vacuum, and what you do or don't do impacts the organization as a whole. One corrupt leader can corrode the functioning of an entire organization. It is imperative that you work in concert with your fellow leaders to do the right thing, at all times. Whatever you do, don't reduce yourself to a stereotype and be part of a good old boys or girls club. Rise above that high school level social system and be a leader among leaders. Just like you owe your team your best, you owe your organization your best as well. You were hired and are being paid to achieve goals. Earn your paycheck. Carry out the responsibilities you are tasked with, whether they are operational or supervisory. Your job is to get the best results possible, with includes the process, the product, and the people. You need to be actively engaged in all three areas on a daily basis. This isn't about you. This is about the team as a whole.

The product is the easy part of the job. You either sell or deliver a service or product. No matter how simple or complex, you will have operational procedures that are necessary to create and distribute the product or service. Your job is to participate in and oversee production and delivery. Do your part well, and make sure your people are doing their part well. That includes collaborating with your internal and external stakeholders, partners, and customers. Be known as the go-to group that treats everyone well, whether they work in the mailroom, the boardroom, or are a member of the public.

The people are the messy part of the job. Sometimes they will bring you joy, sometimes heartache but at the end of the day the journey with them is well worth it. View your team as just one group among many, and strive to help them be their very best and deliver exceptional results.

The process is where things can get really tangled up. It's also an area where you can have a lot of fun creatively solving problems. How you do things is just as important as what you are doing, and why you are doing it. If your process is out of whack, it will throw your people off. Many times, friction between people can be traced back to an operational process that has sticking points, bottlenecks, or other snafus that once identified, are reasonably overcome. Master the art of streamlining the process and you will have added tremendous value to all aspects of the organization. Products / services will move through the system more quickly and easily, people will get along better, barriers to success will be broken down, and you will help ensure that your organization is operating at peak efficiency and effectiveness.

Next up we'll talk about how to achieve this streamlining by focusing on deliverables, the mission, and the culture.

<u>Chapter Seven: Daily Deliverables</u>

You are responsible for results in two areas: your own workload, and the team's. Part of the fun of leadership is producing something of value of your own, and helping your people produce what they are responsible for as well. The overall mission and goals of the organization are usually set at a level above yours. There are typically yearly, quarterly, or monthly objectives that need to be met. Take one extra step above and beyond the norm and break those goals down into daily deliverables for yourself and the team. This is where it becomes critical to play to people's strengths, and position them for success. Match people's skills and personalities with operational needs and you'll have a huge leg up on meeting goals. Minimally acceptable standards will have already been set by other people, so this isn't a matter of figuring out how to do the bare minimum necessary to get by. Don't settle for that! Take your team to the next level by maximizing their talents and opportunities to add as much value as possible to the organization.

Ask the team to help you improve the process and the product, and you will have a group that continually refreshes and renews itself. There will be little chance for boredom, and mischief will be minimized when people are actively engaged not only in doing their basic job, but in helping strengthen the organization as a whole. It's a great mindset for people to be in and stay in during their workday. Far better than hating being there, thinking what they do doesn't really matter, and watching the clock until it is time to go home.

Do the same thing for yourself. Think about how you can add value beyond what you are already accomplishing. Propose projects or new initiatives, figure out how to overcome obstacles, find ways to increase productivity or lower costs. Have fun with this, and spend time thinking about the bigger picture. Set the example and keep yourself engaged in a process of continuous improvement. It will make your job more interesting too. Each day, think about how you can make your team's life operationally easier, both in real time and over the long haul. This is one of the best problem prevention strategies you can use. When people's stress level is minimized and their productivity maximized, they will be free to give their very best to the organization. Be a change agent, and fine tune what you are doing until you have a smoothly operating system in place that allows both you and the team to thrive.

Carefully consider what support and resources you need to improve results. There are a lot of low or no cost resources available online or at your local public library, that can help you think of ways to make things better for yourself and the team. Recognizing, rewarding, and supporting people in their pursuit of organizational goals is one of the most important parts of your job. Make sure that people understand how what they do contributes to the overall accomplishment of the mission. Make sure that everyone feels valued, respected, and included. When you take care of the people, the product, and the process, the daily deliverables take care of themselves.

A Tale of Two Managers Continued

Emma

Emma was keenly aware of her responsibility to the larger organization. In fact, commitment to fulfilling the company mission was part of what got her out of bed in the morning. She loved having her own workload, overseeing the work of others, and being part of a larger executive team that worked hard to increase company profits and provide outstanding customer service. It was a comprehensive and exciting variety of roles she played, and she thoroughly enjoyed each one of them. She had long since mastered her own daily deliverables, but always kept an eye out for improving them. She went a step beyond the norm and rather than just keeping tabs on her people's workloads, she taught them how to track their own results. She taught her people to always work a bit ahead of the curve, so that if they had a rough day for any reason they would not fall behind on their overall goals. Once the team adjusted to this new system, they saw its value and it became an ingrained part of their work process.

Emma also held periodic meetings with the team, where the topic of discussion was for each person to bring in a problem they saw, and at least one potential solution for dealing with it. Together they talked through process, product, and yes sometimes people problems, and came up with a consensus solution to either try, or propose to the higher ups. This exercise had a few primary benefits. First, the team spent their mental energy focused on making things better. This kept them on track and working as a cohesive unit. Second, they learned to respond calmly to problems because they were always in objective solution mode. Third, Emma learned about problems in real time while they were still small and could be solved with the least harsh intervention. As a result, her team became the go-to group for taking the pulse of what was really happening in the company, and for teaching other teams how to solve the problems they were facing. Emma's team had an excellent reputation across the company for adding value far beyond the completion of their basic work assignments.

Jolene

Jolene's focus when she showed up to work every day was doing the bare minimum required. She had been around forever, shuffling from place to place in search of more pay and prestige. That was about the extent of the big picture thinking she engaged in. She was always angling for her next promotion, and spent significant time each day calling in or doing favors for her widespread network of cronies. She was always making some kind of shady deal with one person or another. She cut corners in ways that compromised quality. She produced very little of her own real work. She didn't want her team bothering her any more than absolutely necessary. When they got bored they asked for more or different things to do but she always refused these requests. She caused them a great deal of frustration and stress. Her team tried to work together, but Jolene's volatile personality shut people down and created divisions between them. She handled her own stress poorly, including prescription drug abuse and screaming at people. She went into rages that didn't even make sense, and that were vastly out of proportion to the situation at hand. She was too self-absorbed to notice, and too selfish to care if her team was stressed. She careened her way from reactive episode to reactive episode on almost a daily basis. Although she had attained a high level position, she was bitter about having been passed over for promotion several times. Her reputation preceded her, and she was known for being a problem employee throughout the company. It was well known that she manipulated the process, didn't care at all about the product, and mistreated her people. Few people trusted her. The only reason she didn't lose her job entirely was because her cronies protected her, using the justification that since she was doing the bare minimum she couldn't be asked to do more.

Exercises

✓ Rate each one of your direct report's current stress level on a scale of 1-10. In just a few words, jot down why you think that stress exists (ie family, finances, workload, etc).

_____

_____

_____

_____

✓ If the source of stress is work related, what can you do to fix it? Does the workload need to be rebalanced? Is there a problem individual causing everyone trouble? Is there a process problem that you and the team can tackle together? Is your personal assistance needed in some other way?

_____

_____

_____

_____

✓ If the source of stress is not work related, what support can you offer? Can you provide information about resources in the community? Or does the employee just need to know that you are aware of their situation and care about them?

_____

_____

_____

_____

✓ Now rate your team's current stress level on a scale of 1-10. In a few words, jot down what you think the source of that stress is. What can you do to fix it? Are there common themes between individual stress and group stress (ie disruptive person in the work environment), or is it a temporary/seasonal/normal part of the business cycle?

_____

_____

_____

_____

✓ Next, think about how each person is handling their individual stress. Also think about how the team is handling their group stress. What do you see? Are people starting to crack up under the strain? Are they starting to squabble? Are there other signs of performance or conduct problems on the horizon that can be traced back to too much stress? Or are they handling it well and you know this is just a temporary circumstance they'll quickly and readily bounce back from?

_____

_____

_____

_____

✓ If you think one of your people or the team as a whole is having too much trouble, formulate a stress reduction plan. Or if you think someone has the capacity to go over the edge and behave in a disruptive, volatile, or dangerous way, come up with an intervention plan. Sketch out those plans here.

_____

_____

_____

_____

✓ What else can you do to mitigate individual and group stress? Are there training videos you can show, links to online resources you can provide, or guest speakers you can bring in who specialize in stress reduction?

_____

_____

_____

_____

✓ Finally, do the exercises listed above for your own stress level:
   ○ On a scale of 1-10, what is it?

   _____

   ○ What is the source of the stress?

   _____

   ○ How are you handling it?

   _____

   ○ What is your stress reduction plan?

   _____

   ○ Do you need support or help with getting your stress back under control?

   _____

   ○ If so, what resources will you utilize to do so?

   _____

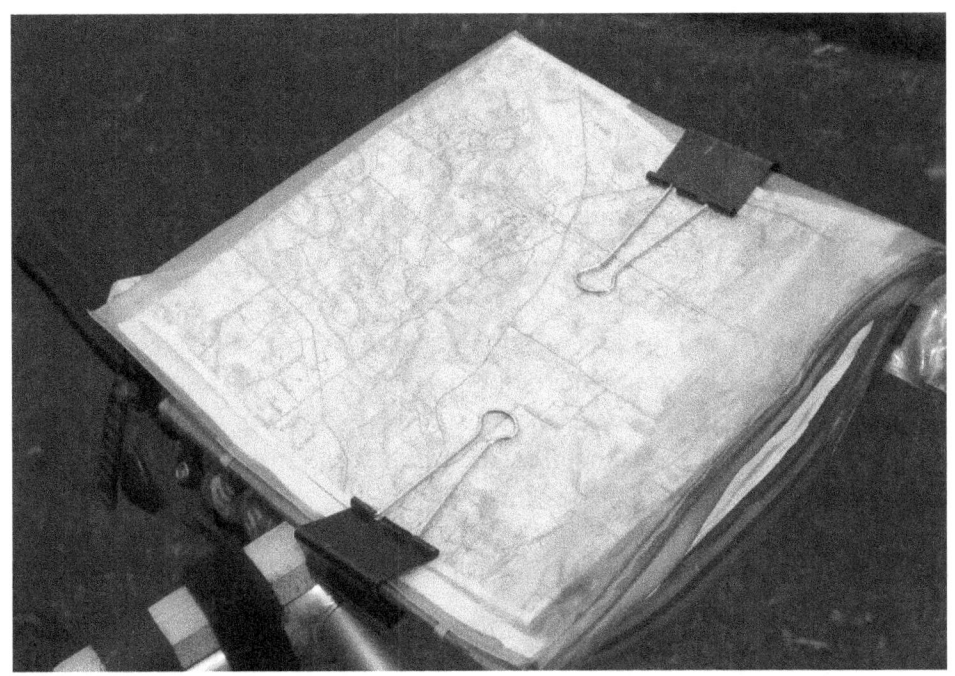

<u>Chapter Eight: Mission Evolution</u>

As a leader, you are not only tasked with fulfilling the mission, it is your responsibility to help evolve it over time. The mission must adapt to internal and external business realities and environments. Today's organizations are called upon more and more to keep up with competitive demands and dwindling resources. Evolve the mission so that you are riding the surf instead of being thrown around by the waves. It only takes one scandal, one bad economic decision, or one breach of public trust to dismantle even the hardiest of companies these days. Robustly defining and regularly updating the mission, and then insisting that every level of the company make mission driven decisions, creates a buffer zone that protects the viability and longevity of the organization. It is also an essential step towards scandal proofing your organization. When a well thought out, carefully vetted, contemporary mission is *the* defining factor in organizational life, it is much harder for anyone to stray off course.

The mission is the reason your organization exists. Your company (or team, or non-profit, etc) was created because someone had a dream, and they had very particular ideas about how those goals should be accomplished. It only makes sense that once an enterprise of any kind is up and running, adjustments will have to be made. One of the healthiest activities any organization can engage in is stepping back regularly to ask "is this still where we want to go and how we want to get there?" Refining the mission as you gain experience in the marketplace (or on the ballfield or in the boardroom) makes good sense and allows you to proactively adapt to changing circumstances.

As a leader you have three mission statements to concern yourself with: yours, the team's, and the organization's. First, if you don't have your own mission statement for your leadership in your current role, you are doing a disservice to yourself. One of the most important things you can do for the team is to decide for yourself what your leadership career is all about, why you are doing it, what you value along the way, and how you plan to accomplish good outcomes. Second, conduct exercises with your team to choose as a group what your mission, vision, values, and strategic plan will be. Don't just adopt what the organization's stated positions are, craft your own in alignment with the greater goals. Discuss and decide how you want your group to function, what you're trying to accomplish, and how you'll treat each other, along with anything else your team values enough to declare and then be held accountable to. Then meet periodically to talk about the progress the team is making towards accomplishing both group and organizational goals. Specifically discuss the mission, vision, values and strategic plans and whether or not you are living up to them. Adjust as necessary, and keep moving forward together.

A Tale of Two Managers Continued

Emma

For years, Emma had been using her own personal leadership mission, vision, and values statement. She updated them at least annually to reflect how she had grown, current environmental conditions, and what she wanted to accomplish next. These living documents were a beacon to her on the hardest days, and guided her decisions and behavior every day. She worked hard to live up to the standards she had set for herself.

It was only natural that she would utilize this same process to keep her team on track. They blocked off time at least yearly to sit down together and talk through, point by point, every line item contained within the mission, vision, and values statement. They were not afraid to discard anything that was no longer necessary, or that no longer served their greatest good. They were enthusiastic about adding creative, innovative line items if they were feasible to include. They honored the core mission and values of their organization, and built their group specific goals around them. As part of their annual review of the documents, they talked candidly about how well they as a group had achieved their objectives. Some line items were retained so that they had another chance to get them right. Others proved beyond their control and were deleted so that other, more achievable objectives could take their place. As the years passed, the team became proficient in setting and achieving goals. Their standards were higher than what was required, and both their culture and results were envied by teams who had less progressive leaders.

Jolene

Jolene had no vision for her career, just a jealous desire to grab all that she could for all long as she could. She saw people much like chess pieces to maneuver around so she could win. She didn't have a mission statement of her own, and rolled her eyes at the one her organization had posted on the wall. She couldn't have cared less about what goals anyone was attempting to reach. Her values consisted of whatever gained her the greatest advantage in the moment. If it took lying to get what she wanted, she was fine with that. If she thought intimidation would clear her path of obstacles, she engaged in it without even a flicker of hesitation. She did not live by principle, and was easily swayed by circumstances. Her logic was faulty, and her emotions were barely under control. Not exactly the kind of leader who inspires confidence and hope. Her team had serious morale problems, and was fractured along the fault lines of those who felt they could ride Jolene's coattails to success for themselves, and people who actually wanted to do the job and help the organization succeed. She sowed seeds of division among people, and was enormously threatened by anyone under her who showed any kind of leadership potential. The truth was, several other people could do her job better than she could. They knew it, and she knew it. Observing her, one could only conclude that her mission was to destroy the competition. Her team performed seriously below their potential. Whether or not they were meeting minimum standards was a matter of serious debate within the organization. Jolene was either oblivious to this or didn't care. She felt invincible. Because she had no wisdom or maturity, she didn't comprehend that she was leaving herself enormously vulnerable to the changes that would inevitably come. She might be resting in the shade of her cronies now, but if ever there came a time when there was a changing of the guard, her chances of survival were scant at best. She had been living far too crazy for far too long, and people had long ago written her off as a lost cause.

Exercises

- ✓ Do a mission, vision, and values statement for your own leadership career.
- ✓ Do a mission, vision, and values statement with your team. Make reviewing organizational statements about these topics a part of the process for everyone.
- ✓ Do a strategic plan with your team, in terms of what you would like to accomplish together as a group. Ideas include cross-training, special assignments, and productivity goals.

<u>Chapter Nine: Keeper of the Cultural Flame</u>

The single biggest aspect of your organization that will make or break its success is the culture. Healthy cultures facilitate people thriving and organizational objectives being met. Dysfunctional cultures erode people's well-being and stop goals from being accomplished. Healthy cultures breathe life into the team and the mission. Dysfunctional cultures offer only destruction and decay.

You need to create a healthy culture and protect it with vigilance. Even if your larger organization does not offer the best culture to work in, make sure your own team has the benefit of a healthy culture within the group.

What is a healthy culture? One in which the mission is the focus, the values are for the benefit of all, the vision advances the common good, and the work environment is safe – including emotionally safe – for everyone. It allows each person to be who they are, while still treating other people respectfully. It establishes ground rules for behavior and then holds people accountable to them. It establishes expectations for productivity and then holds people accountable to those too. It establishes what the organization believes in and the role it is working to fulfill in society, and then holds people accountable to those ideals. It is an organization in which true teamwork takes place, and each person contributes to the mission and the environment in positive, value added ways. It is a place with an energy of vitality and growth. It is a place where people are emotionally and physically safe. In today's environment of workplace violence, the importance of establishing and maintaining safety for your team cannot be overstated.

Dysfunctional cultures have one hallmark feature: there is some kind of poison running through the system. That poison may be one person who is allowed to disrupt the work environment without consequences. The poison may be a good old boys or good old girls club that squelches other people's opportunities for success. The poison may be one really bad leader who has a stranglehold on the power in the organization. The poison may be immature behavior or shirking of duties that goes unchecked. The poison may be skimming money off of company accounts. The poison may be ripping off the public, or defrauding the stakeholders. The poison may be abuse of those you are charged with looking after. The poison may be addiction that interferes with the functioning of the organization. The poison may be outright corruption. Whatever form the poison takes, it will contaminate the culture and nothing good will survive in that toxic soil. A toxic culture will damage people in their heart, mind, and spirit. It will corrode their careers and seep into their personal lives. It will claim marriages as its victims, and spill over into child and animal abuse. It will compromise community and diminish dreams that would have otherwise come true. It will steal hope one piece at a time until someone takes their own life. Do you really want to be responsible for those kinds of consequences? Because if you are causing or allowing poison to flow through your workplace, you will be.

As a leader, the culture starts with you. Leaders set the tone. It is your job to maintain standards. A team is only as strong as its weakest leader. If you are a leader of other leaders, you'll be responsible for the impact they have on their teams and the organization. There is nothing more important in your relationship with your other leaders than holding them accountable for being healthy, mature, functional human beings. If they are not, they will damage the team, violate organizational values and drag down the mission. In the worst case scenarios, they will mire your organization in controversy and scandal. Ultimately, they may cause the organization to go under because of negative press or massive public backlash. None of the worst scandals in recent memory happened in a flash. They grew over time, with little misdeeds being ignored. That didn't help the offenders. It emboldened them. They took more chances and made even worse choices. Until one day they crossed the line, and there was no turning back. When their day of reckoning came, they took down a lot of people with them. If you are aware of violations at your workplace, it is absolutely imperative that you take action to put a stop to them before they spiral out of control. Don't think it can't happen to you, or that you know the offender better than that. Not using the full power of your intellect to think through the situation is an invitation to be exploited by the very people you think you are protecting. Any friendship or other tie you may have with someone who is poisoning the system is not worth the risk of you bearing the consequences of their misdeeds. The stakes are far too high to blindly trust or be too weak to correct the situation.

Once you've established a healthy culture, guard it like a sentry at the gate. Do not allow poison in any form to ever flow through the system. If you detect it, eliminate it. You are not doing anyone any good if you are not holding people accountable in this critical area. The culture is for the benefit of all, from the janitor to the CEO, to the stakeholders and the customers. A healthy culture requires active tending. Do not allow dysfunctional undercurrents to develop in your organization, they quickly turn to poison that contaminates everything it comes into contact with.

If you truly want to be an awesome leader, this is where the journey is won or lost for you. You either create a healthy culture and enjoy tremendous success, or you cause or allow a toxic culture and suffer through squalid conditions. It doesn't matter how bold your vision, how sound your values, how inspiring your mission, or how elegant your strategic plan. If you don't get the culture piece of the equation right, you have failed.

A Tale of Two Managers Continued

Emma

Emma simply wouldn't tolerate poison in her work culture. She would root it out like an errant dandelion that took up residence in her yard. She was keenly alert to undercurrents and didn't allow them the opportunity to take hold. She was known for being calm and reasonable, but when it came to toxic dynamics she was fierce. She would work with people all day long on performance issues, stand by them through hard personal times, coach them as they grew past any areas of immaturity, but heaven help them if they ever violated the culture. They learned a quick and painful lesson in those instances, which was that Emma would protect the team over the individual every time that choice had to be made. She took this aspect of her responsibility extremely seriously. As a matter of principle, she passionately believed that every person deserved a healthy, productive place to work. She would never allow her people's emotional or physical safety to be compromised.

Emma also wouldn't tolerate corruption on her watch. She would never participate in the schemes of her peers to create a cottage industry of personal gain. She would address or report poison running through the system every time she saw it. People thrived in such a healthy environment. They were highly productive and contributed greatly to mission accomplishment. She was personally responsible for the organization's ability to intervene in several incidents before any kind of scandal could gain traction. She helped create new company wide protocols for assessing and dealing with problems before they had a toxic impact. She was at peace with how she treated her team, the results they achieved, and the environment they enjoyed working in every day. She knew that her positive impact would help provide for the team and protect the organization long after she retired. She knew that her coaching and mentoring had influenced a significant number of people to choose to grow, to stand up and take leadership, and to do the right thing. She knew that the day she chose to hang up the cleats, she would be forever grateful and regard these achievements as one of the greatest blessings of her life. She had indeed made the difference she had set out to make.

Jolene

A great deal of poison in the organizational culture could be traced back to Jolene. She exhibited tremendous immaturity, dysfunctional thinking, and malicious behavior. She caused enough of her own problems. But even worse, she was a leader responsible for other leaders. Many concerns had been reported to her but all she did was shriek and stomp and malign the

82

messenger. She didn't know or care if the reports were true. Anytime she was told to investigate a particularly serious incident, she simply propped her feet up on her desk, made a couple of phone calls to chat, and called it good. Then she reported back to her higher ups that all was well. Until one day when her carefully constructed web of lies ensnared her. A scandal in her organization that had been brewing for years blew up. Police were on the scene, and media vans streamed in from all over the country. People did not hesitate to offer up Jolene by name as someone who knew what was happening and could have prevented the incident but didn't. Jolene was mortified. She had always been able to lie and hide her misdeeds before. But now she was being tried and convicted in the court of public opinion and the jury was not amused. Jolene faced a life-changing crisis. Take accountability and have a slim chance of saving herself, or find herself behind bars. It wasn't looking good for her, and virtually no one believed she would actually choose to turn things around. She had the blood of a lot of people on her hands, and there were people – including Jolene – who would never be the same after that fateful day.

<u>Exercises</u>

✓ Gauge the health of your workplace culture on a scale of 1 to 10.

_____

_____

_____

_____

✓ Explain the impact you think the culture is having on people.

_____

_____

_____

_____

✓ List any sources of poison that you may see.

_____

_____

_____

_____

✓ Describe the damage you either know the poison has caused, or has the potential to cause.

_____

_____

_____

_____

_____

_____

✓ List the options you will consider for dealing with each source of poison.

_____

_____

_____

_____

_____

_____

✓ List the people you will consult to help you deal with each source of poison.

_____

✓ Name just one thing you will start doing to improve the culture.

_____

✓ Name just one thing you will stop doing to improve the culture.

_____

✓ Describe what you are going to do with your own team to improve the culture.

_____

_____

_____

_____

<u>Part Four: Leadership of the Community</u>

Leaders hold an incredibly powerful role in society. They are highly influential in the lives of many people. They are well positioned to protect and advance the common good. Their skills allow them to make a significant contribution beyond their official leadership role, whether it is in sports, business, politics, religion or any other area. Communities need good leaders at the table making decisions for their future. Churches need good leaders to assist the pastors with creating a strong and sustainable strategic plan. Youth and adult sports programs are in need of good leaders to coach and manage them. Politicians need good leaders to help organize and educate them on the myriad of issues they need to contend with. No matter what your area of interest in life, there is a need for your leadership skills. There are a lot of great organizations out there that can't afford consultants or highly experienced leaders. They are getting by on volunteers who care deeply but may lack the specialized skills to help bring their vision into reality. You can help them take it to the next level and make a profound difference in their ability to accomplish the mission. Volunteering your time and talent, and leveraging your connections can play a vital role in the viability of an organization that is helping meet critical community needs. This can be one of the most rewarding things you do. You don't check your leadership skills at the door when you leave work at the end of the day. Leadership isn't just what you do, it's who you are. You can be an answer to someone's prayer by partnering with them, if even for a brief time.

A final note. As a leader, you will have more visibility in the community than other people. Learn how to accept this. People will always be watching you, looking up to you, and observing how you handle things. Make sure that there is congruence between your personal and professional worlds. This brings us back to the beginning of the book, when we talked about the importance of being an integrated, whole, functional person. If you have a steady baseline of behavior that people can count on no matter whether you are at work, at home, or out in the community, you will quickly become a trusted and highly respected leader. The more you attain self-mastery and wisdom, the more you will solidify an excellent reputation. Cherish this.

Chapter Ten: Collaborative Advancement

One of the easiest ways to get involved in giving back to the community is to participate in collaborative advancement. This can be as simple as giving $5/month to a worthy organization who is doing work in your area of interest. There is an incredibly diverse array of wonderful causes out there that are in need of support and every little bit helps. Three examples from my own life in the last year are Door County Sled Dogs (www. doorcountysleddogs.com), Oceans of Fun (www.oceansoffun.org), and Soldier's Angels (www.soldiersangels.org). Door County Sled Dogs are a team of rescues who have an educational mission and are run entirely by volunteers. Oceans of Fun takes in sea lion and seal rescues, and educates people about these wonderful marine mammals and their habitat. Among other things, Soldier's Angels sends letters and care packages to our troops. I chose to support the sled dog team and Oceans because I deeply love animals, and their missions are so unique that I was immediately enthralled. I chose Soldier's Angels because they are also filling a much needed gap, and I am incredibly appreciative of our military and the many sacrifices they and their families make for the rest of us. The point is, those are causes that I am highly interested in so it was easy and meaningful to make those commitments. The money makes a difference for them, and it is very meaningful to me to have developed a relationship with the folks running these organizations. I know I am a part of something greater that serves the community in a unique, beautiful way.

I do not say this to brag, but to make a point: if I gave you the list of all the places I've contributed to financially, or volunteered for in my life, it would run for pages. I have never been wealthy. At times in my life I have been very poor. But I always found a way to contribute towards the greater good. One of my primary business motivations is to make more so I can give more. To whom much is given, much is required (Luke 12:48, King James Bible). The point is, no matter how much or how little time or money you have, there is a way you can help that will make an impact. It will be one of the most rewarding things you ever do.

If a monthly commitment does not appeal to you, there are plenty of other project based opportunities to contribute. Habitat for Humanity (www.habitat.org), short mission trips, or volunteering at a senior center fundraiser are just a few examples of brief commitments of time, with minimal expense (if any at all), that makes a big difference to those you help.

If projects don't appeal to you either, then there is always disaster relief. When tragedy strikes, resources can be strained to their limit. A lot of us giving a little time or money can go a long ways towards overcoming a tragedy. If all you ever give in your life is disaster relief, you've still made a big impact.

How the Stories End

Ichabod spent his life taking rather than giving. He died the way he lived, angry and reckless. The ripple impact he left behind was negative. He had hurt a lot of people in his life, and those folks had to heal and regain their equilibrium before they could go on to make the difference they were born to make. He delayed good people doing good for their communities because of the damage he had caused.

Mrs. Rogers finally had her judgment day, and it wasn't pretty. All the pain she had enjoyed inflicting on others boomeranged right back on her. Her anger ate her up from the inside out until her health completely crashed. By then it was too late for her to reverse a lot of the damage, and she suffered greatly for many years. Too weak and sick to do the things she wanted, she spent her days hobbling from room to room in her house. Those who loved and cared about her had long since given up on ever seeing her change. Their mistrust was well founded because she never did get honest about her problems. Her life never did improve, and she grew into a frail, bitter old woman.

To her credit, Jolene did manage to take a good long look at herself when it became clear that outrunning her consequences was no longer possible. She had left a lot of wreckage in her path, but there was a defining moment in time when she decided enough was enough and she wanted to live right. She did not have an overnight or miraculous turnaround. She had to face some pretty harsh penalties for her previous behavior, but she stayed the course and kept up with the new way of living. Over time she worked through her issues, grew into a good enough leader, did right by her organization, and became a valuable and respected member of her community. She volunteered and financially supported a few carefully selected organizations in her town, and they were grateful for her help. She was eventually able to make a major difference in her community, and it helped make up for all the hurt she had caused before. She felt really good about redeeming herself in this way.

Emma continued to grow in maturity, skills, and responsibility throughout her long and prosperous career. She was actively involved in her community, giving financially, volunteering her time, and sharing her talents with carefully vetted organizations. She gained a reputation in the community as a leader who cared about more than money or prestige, who genuinely wanted to resolve problems, meet needs, and fill gaps. She never compromised her career, family life, or health as she engaged in the community, but over time she gave significantly and a lot of people and causes were better off because of her. Her ripple impact was huge, which was how she had wanted to finish her race.

Exercises

✓ What is your preference for giving back to the community?
- o Ongoing commitment of time and/or money
- o Brief project based contributions
- o Disaster relief

_____

_____

_____

_____

_____

_____

_____

_____

_____

✓ Based on your preference, pick one cause to give time, talent, or treasure to in this next year.

_____

_____

_____

_____

_____

_____

_____

_____

_____

Chapter Eleven: Life Altering Experiences

As a general rule, leaders make more money than a lot of other folks do. This incredible blessing is not to be taken lightly, or hoarded for selfish pursuits. Leaders have the ability to provide major blessings that profoundly alters the course of someone's future. At least once in your life, do something amazing for someone. Really, truly, over the top awesome. The kind of thing that catapults them towards their dreams in a quantum leap they could never accomplish on their own. Do this without fanfare and with no expectation of anything in return for yourself. Do it because you can and because it changes the course of history for at least two people: the recipient, and yourself. You will not be unchanged by this process.

Here are some examples. Start an emergency fund at your vet's office for families who can't pay for necessary medical care for their beloved pets. Create a new scholarship even if it is small at first. Start a new sports program that gives people who wouldn't otherwise have the opportunity to participate, the experience of team play. Pay for music, art, or other types of lessons for a kid growing up in hard circumstances. Send a kid to a summer camp in their area of interest. Finance a local church's youth mission trip. Pay off a single mom's car. Mentor or tutor someone. Volunteer to lead a major community initiative such as reducing homelessness. Offer strategic planning services to a non-profit at no charge. The opportunities are endless. Ask only one thing of the recipient: that they will become all they are meant to be and will do something really good for someone else someday. This isn't just throwing a pebble into the pond, it's heaving a boulder into it. The ripple impact will be massive and far reaching.

How the Stories End

Ichabod squandered the opportunity to be of use and value to his fellow man. His life-altering experiences left people in tremendous pain. Some of them would never fully recover, and their ability to be of use and value was greatly diminished.

Mrs. Rogers had more money than most, but frittered it away on momentary pleasures that never truly made her happy. As her health declined and she was no longer able to work, her income dropped drastically. She had even less energy to go out and about. She couldn't have volunteered her time or given money now even if she had wanted to. Which she didn't. She still hated everyone. She had been selfish with her money and all the good in the world she could have done with it died before it ever saw the light of day. Properly used, without hurting herself at all, she could have planted seeds with her money and watched them grow into a changed world. She could have helped fund a lot of dreams but it was not to be.

Jolene got this part really right. As a way of making up for her misdeeds in the past, Jolene chose to do one life altering experience for someone each year. As time passed, she helped resolve desperate situations, provided business assistance, and mentored a significant number of youth in her church. She knew nothing would ever erase what she had done wrong in the past, but she was determined to be a good steward of her blessings now.

Emma kept her eyes open for ways she could be a significant blessing to others. When she heard of a need, or saw an opportunity, she would carefully consider it and pray about it. She wanted to do at least a few amazing things for people before her time on earth was through. She waited for situations that could be met no other way than through her assistance. She bought a car for a widower who was struggling to make ends meet and had to travel significant mileage for work. She made a down payment on a home for a young family who was just starting out. She made up the difference in college expenses for a kid who worked two jobs to survive. She provided her local senior center with pro bono assistance for creating a sustainable financial plan. She never broadcast what she had done. She knew and understood the life changing difference she had made, and that was enough.

Exercises

Figure out someone you can do something amazing for. Or an organization you can have a major impact on. If you can't afford the money, then give time. If you can't do it now then stay alert for opportunities to do so. You are making a huge commitment of resources, so make sure it's the right person/place and the right time. This exercise will change both you and the recipient for good.

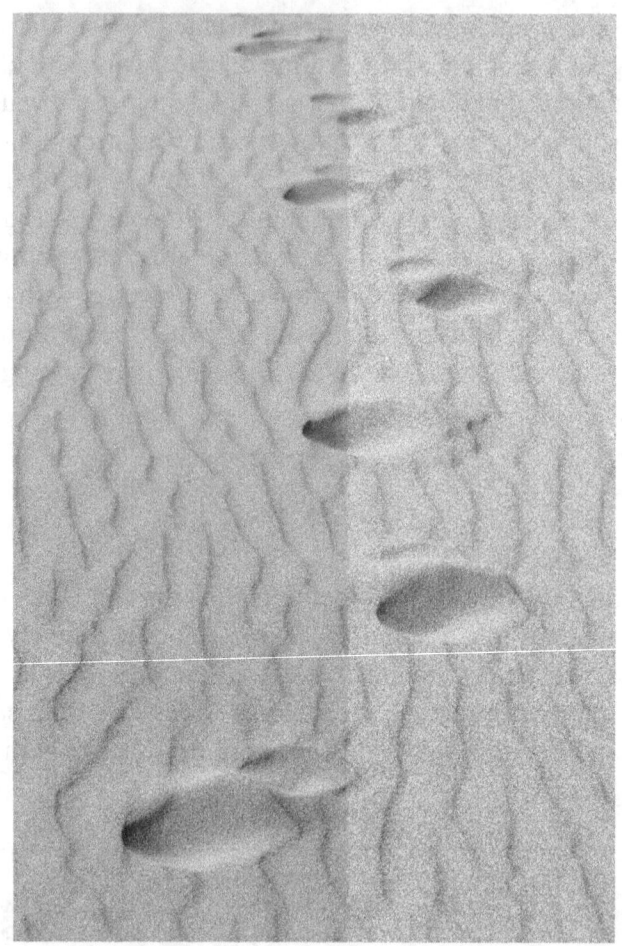

<u>Chapter Twelve: Leaving a Powerful Legacy</u>

You will leave a legacy whether you want to or not. You have control over whether it is positive or negative. How do you want to be remembered? Do you want to be known as someone who wasted their life and held other people back? Or do you want to be known as someone who took really good care of their family and community? How do you want the world to be different because you lived? Do you want only a string of broken dreams left in your wake, or do you want to have living memorials walking around who credit you with helping turn their life around? It is entirely up to you.

Life is a precious God-given gift. It can be over in a heartbeat. We need to be wise stewards of the time that we are granted. Make each day count.

Make contributions that will long outlive your personal presence on this planet. Make decisions that in the final analysis, left your very best on the field of life. The rest of us are counting on you.

How the Stories End

Ichabod left a legacy of shattered dreams and shattered hearts. He never took his life seriously. He never spent time thinking about the impact he was having. Many people he wounded had to spend time overcoming the legacy of pain he had forced upon them. He overpowered people in all areas of his life, trampling them into the ground just for sport. His immaturity cost him his life, and he never got a second chance to make things right.

Mrs. Rogers created a legacy of pain. She had sacrificed countless people in her quest to live a rogue lifestyle. They would eventually bounce back and go on to great accomplishments. She tried to deny them a future, but she only managed to delay it. The worst impact of all however, was on her own life. She was in constant physical pain and emotional distress. Her hatred had poisoned her body, mind, and spirit. She found joy in nothing, not even in the simple pleasures of life. She was drowning in debt. She had no one to care for her or look after her, because her cruelty had long ago driven away everyone from her life. Her loneliness was immense. The worst legacy of all was the one she left for herself. While others rose from the ashes she had caused in their life, she was never able to escape from the mud pit she would wallow in for the rest of her days. It was a miserable existence.

Jolene woke up one day and realized she wouldn't live forever. She thought a lot about the mistakes she had made, and they weighed heavily on her mind. She was personally responsible for broken homes and broken lives. She knew those people would never be the same because of her, and it was not something she was proud of. She decided that her legacy would be an example of how one person could turn their life around and still make a difference. She committed to do everything within her power to finish well. She became an exemplary leader, known for her integrity and compassion. She managed to save her marriage and not lose custody of her kids. She was working diligently to help her husband's dreams come true, and help her kids have a great start to their adult life. She started a foundation, small at first but it grew over time, mentoring troubled youth in her community. The vast majority of those kids went on to highly successful lives, and were making a difference in their own communities. She was exceedingly grateful that her ripple impact was finally a positive one. She was an inspiration for those who had rough starts or really messed things up. Her life demonstrated that redemption was possible, and this one thing alone provided people with a lot of hope.

Emma wanted to be an impact player in her generation. She wanted to make a huge difference in the world. She pursued the dreams God put in her heart with zeal and enthusiasm. Her results were not perfect but they were awesome. Her professional legacy consisted of a lengthy list of accomplishments. Chief among them was her successful effort to gather a team of people to overhaul the culture and values of her company. Policies, procedures, and protocols were put into place because of her relentless lobbying for taking better care of people. Her personal legacy was just as much a reflection of the quality of how she lived her life. Her family cherished her, and she provided for and protected them extremely well. Her community celebrated her. She had a vision for meeting needs, and the programs she created would long outlive her. Many people's lives had been changed, and her legacy was secure.

Exercise

Take your time with this exercise, and give it careful thought. Your legacy is not a topic to think through quickly or lightly. It deserves serious consideration. Once you choose what you want it to be, or at least that you want it to be positive, it will inform and guide your decisions for the rest of your life.

✓ Describe what you want your professional legacy to be.

_____

_____

_____

_____

_____

_____
_____
_____
_____
_____
_____
_____
_____
_____
_____
_____
_____
_____

✓ Describe what you want your personal legacy to be.

_____
_____
_____
_____
_____
_____
_____
_____
_____
_____
_____
_____
_____
_____
_____
_____
_____
_____
_____

Conclusion: Call to Action

Leaders my leaders! What about you? Are you willing to put in the hard work of truly leading yourself rather than being led by the shifting winds of circumstance? Do you care enough about your team to legitimately do right by them, rather than exploiting them for your personal gain? Will you become a vigilant keeper of your organization's mission and culture, rather than leaving it haphazardly to chance? Will you become a leader among leaders in your generation, and share your gifts with the community? Answer the call and make the decision to take the journey to awesomeness today. There's no time to lose, your team is counting on you!

Now that you've worked your way through all the exercises in the book, sketch out your master strategy for becoming awesome in the following areas:

✓ Self

      o Personal maturity

      _____
      _____
      _____
      _____

      o Integrated wholeness

      _____
      _____
      _____
      _____

      o Sustainable pace

      _____
      _____
      _____
      _____

✓ Team

    o Interpersonal excellence

_____
_____
_____
_____

    o Strategically developing others

_____
_____
_____
_____

    o The art of consequences

_____
_____
_____
_____

✓ Organization

    o Daily deliverables

_____
_____
_____
_____

    o Mission evolution

_____
_____
_____
_____

o Cultural flame

_____

_____

_____

_____

✓ Community

    o Collaborative advancement

_____

_____

_____

_____

    o Life-altering experiences

_____

_____

_____

_____

    o Legacy

_____

_____

_____

_____

About the Author

Deb Holland's professional credentials include leadership positions in both the private and public sectors, as well as a Bachelor of Social Work degree from the University of Montana, a Master of Social Work from Walla Walla College, a Master of Public Administration from the University of Montana, and a PhD in Interdisciplinary Studies from the University of Montana. She also maintains an active Licensed Clinical Social Worker credential in Wisconsin.

Holland's subject matter expertise in leadership and creating healthy workplaces makes her a sought after speaker. She is passionate about helping people have the best work life possible so they can find the elusive balance necessary to enjoy their life, take good care of their families, make a significant contribution to our world, and become all that God created them to be. She has devoted the rest of her life to helping leaders get it right for all of us, so that our workplaces become healthy and our workforce thrives. We spend too much of our lives at work to accept anything less.

Holland would love to hear from you. Please reach out to her at www.debhollandlcsw.com. Connect with her on social media. Check back

often for the latest value added content she enjoys producing for her audience. Above all, Holland wishes you peace and abundant success on your journey. Now, go be awesome!

© Annie Rubens

About the Photographer Annie Rubens

Annie's life-long love of photography spurred her into launching Rubens Photography in Missoula, Montana in 1995. She was an impact player in her market, specializing in weddings, seniors, family portraits and producing custom commercial images for a variety of projects. Her photography was featured as the cover image for the *Missoulian Brides & Grooms* guide from 1995-2005, and she produced forty unique portraits of authors for the Women's Club book *Spirit & Strength*. In one year at the University of Maryland School of Nursing Annie's work was utilized for advertising, website, portraits, events and media publications. Credits included the *Baltimore Sun, Nursing Spectrum, Advance for Nurses, American Nurse Today, The Voice*, and *Nursing Magazine*.

After relocating to her hometown of Madison, WI in 2007, she focused on other interests including hot yoga, dog agility and competing in sprint distance triathlons. *Make Your Destiny Your Reality* reignited her love of photography when she was challenged to produce a highly specific shot list to illustrate the book. She rose to the challenge, immersing herself once again into the thrill of capturing just the right image for the concepts conveyed in each chapter. She had so much fun producing every quirky shot she decided to launch the second evolution of her business. She currently specializes in producing quality custom images for specific projects and invites you to contact her to begin a conversation about how she can help bring your vision to life.

You can reach her at www.debhollandlcsw.com.

About Spot-On-Graphics, Fran Schiesl

After graduating in 2005 with a Bachelor of Science degree in Communications with a Graphic Design emphasis from the University of Wisconsin-Platteville, I moved to St. Joseph Missouri for my first job in the printing industry. That experience included time spent learning the ins-and-outs of a printing plant, including perfect binding, foil stamping and die cutting, all components that come into play when ensuring a design prints as it should.

"My background in the print industry really made me aware of how projects go from screen to print. I'm privy to what works and what doesn't when it comes to assuring a high-quality print job, something critical to a successful design experience."

Because the print process plays an immense role in how a finished product looks, this expertise sets Spot-On-Graphics apart from many freelance designers. Fran has deep knowledge of how to properly layout items – such as folders, brochures and other specialty products – to ensure they meet the client's expectations, from concept to completion. With over nine years of experience in the print industry, she has the skills to help your business succeed.

WEBSITE:
www.spot-on-graphics.com

EMAIL:
design@spot-on-graphics.com